The Human Touch in Educational Leadership

A Postpositivist Approach to Understanding Educational Leadership

Robert H. Palestini

A SCARECROWEDUCATION BOOK

The Scarecrow Press, Inc.
Lanham, Maryland, and Oxford
2003

A SCARECROWEDUCATION BOOK

Published in the United States of America
by Scarecrow Press, Inc.
A Member of the Rowman & Littlefield Publishing Group
4720 Boston Way, Lanham, Maryland 20706
www.scarecroweducation.com

PO Box 317, Oxford, OX2 9RU, UK

British Library Cataloguing in Publication Information Available

Library of Congress Cataloging-in-Publication Data
Palestini, Robert H.
  The human touch in educational leadership : a postpositivist approach
to understanding educational leadership / Robert H. Palestini.
    p. cm.
"A ScarecrowEducation book."
Includes bibliographical references and index.
  ISBN 0-8108-4515-6 (cloth : alk. paper) — ISBN 0-8108-4516-4 (pbk. :
alk. paper)
  1. Educational leadership—United States—Philosophy. 2. School
management and organization—United States—Philosophy. 3. Positivism.
I. Title.
  LB2805 .P289 2003
  371.2—dc21   2002010301

∞™ The paper used in this publication meets the minimum requirements of
American National Standard for Information Sciences—Permanence of
Paper for Printed Library Materials, ANSI/NISO Z39.48-1992.
Manufactured in the United States of America.

Contents

Introduction: The Human Touch in Educational Administration   1

1   Educational Leadership   5

2   The Positivist/Functionalist Approach to Leadership   12

3   Critical Theory and Leadership   23

4   Educational Administration as a Moral Science   34

5   The Ignatian Vision   40

6   Implications for Organizational Development   50

7   Implications for Institutional Change   95

8   Educational Choice and Vouchers: A Case Study   138

Index   169

About the Author   172

The Human Touch in Educational Administration

A POSITIVIST APPROACH TO UNDERSTANDING EDUCATIONAL LEADERSHIP

Recently, the fields of organizational theory and administrative theory have come under question. The scientific rigor of each has been questioned, as has their ability to contribute meaningfully to the understanding of human affairs. Indeed, the current trend in organizational and administrative theory is to move away from the technical and quantitative emphases so characteristic of the management and organizational sciences, in favor of a more culturally relevant approach that builds on culture and politics.

The science of administration that Frederick Taylor espoused early in the twentieth century demonstrates an insensitivity to culture and politics. Even the human-relations advocates who discovered the Hawthorne Effect did not anticipate the impact of culture and politics on management theory. Instead, the science of administration attempts to abstract from something called "leadership behavior" sets of regularities, predictions, and lawlike statements that subjugate any more subtle distinction about the nature of organization and administration. The science of administration, and much of organizational theory, has really been a science of management, that is, how managers can set in motion certain technical procedures that result in the satisfactory performance and increased motivation of employees. An examination of any introductory text to educational administration would bear this out; culture, politics, morals, and ethics receive, at best, very little attention.

This is especially inadequate for institutions that influence our lives as almost nothing else does. The school, as a social institution, has tremendous impact on a person's life. School is more than simply a class to attend or a degree to be attained; rather, it is a living statement, of culture and of values, that forms a part of the fabric of every social member. This text intends to present the reflective administrative practitioner with a set of issues, concerns, and problems that have been sorely neglected up to now. It explores the development of the human touch in educational administration.

Traditional accounts of administrative theory often exclude or ignore qualitative research because it does not subscribe to a positivistic way of viewing the universe. This scholarship is critical in its efforts, questioning the basic assumptions of administrative theory and linking it to the practice that evolves. We present here, then, just such a critically informed viewpoint of administration, one that attempts to link administrative practice to social, cultural, political, and ethical issues. However, it is an integrated approach in that it does not throw the baby out with the bath water. It retains many of the positivistic principles that are important to effective administration.

An administrator must deal with technical issues, like how to moti-vate staff and communicate effectively and how to resolve conflict. In these instances, the use of positivistic theory is quite appropriate and even encouraged. However, the essence of an administrator's work is not technical; rather, it involves the establishment of a community and a culture within the organization and the development of an organiza-tion's self-reflective ability to analyze its purpose and goals. In these re-sponsibilities, we are suggesting that positivist theory be supplemented with a critical, and even a moral approach to educational administration and leadership. In summary we are suggesting the use of positivist the-ory informed by critical theory and the Ignatian vision of educational administration and leadership.

Therefore, in this text, I will be concerned not only with the smooth oper-ation of the school or school system, but also with how administration con-tributes to the type of society we have and in what ways it impedes or en-hances our cultural ideals and values. These are difficult questions, but one must address them to be a truly reflective and effective administrator and leader. Of prime concern, then, is the critical analysis of both administration and education that is a basic ingredient of reform.

A critical analysis is premised on an understanding of the relationship of theory to practice. Educational and other administrators are distinguished by their commitment to everyday practice. However, many practitioners disdain theory. Theory is what we study in our colleges and universities, some say. It bears no relation to the real world. Yet, it can be noted that all practice derives from theory, whether that theory is intuitively developed over the course of a career or more formally developed through individual scholarship or course of study. And, theory is the primary way of correcting failed practice.

Parenthetically, when I use the term *theory* in this book, we do not use it only in the dictionary sense, whereby theory predicts outcomes, as in a scientific theory. Here, I also use theory as a way of looking at things, as a lens through which certain behaviors and procedures are analyzed. Thus, this text is based on the notion that human affairs are not entirely predictable; that discourse and analysis are inevitable and desirable; that there is no one best system; that we are in a constant state of evolution and change. There are competing theories and competing practices, and it is our role as reflective administrators, individuals of action, to sort through them in order to come up with strategies and courses of action that do justice to our values and beliefs. A positivist view is important for the practical application of positivist principles and helps us deal with and anticipate many of the day-to-day exigencies of our job. However, critical theory is also necessary because it encourages us to view events in historical perspective, to doubt the validity of received truth, and to continue our search for more adequate solutions to our problems. Finally, the Ignatian vision, which was developed by Ignatius of Loyola in the sixteenth century, rounds out a multidimensional, integrated approach to looking at schooling, in general, and educational administration, in particular.

Thus, the material presented to the administrator and the student of administration in this volume is intended to challenge and to question. It attempts to motivate the aspiring administrator and the student of administration in education first to formulate assumptions and ways of thinking through the lens of positivism and, then, to challenge the assumptions through the lens of critical theory. It is designed, finally, to give a larger social context to the idea of administration through the lens of the Ignatian vision so that what we do can make a difference.

Theoretical approaches, such as these, are particularly helpful in successfully implementing change. It has been said that effecting change in education is like making a U-turn with the QE II. I am here to say that it does not have to be this way. Models of change and reform in education have been premised on positivistic notions of how change occurs: setting up a planning committee, developing strategies, convincing gatekeepers, and implementing the change. This has not worked well, mostly because change does not occur in such a planned and rational fashion. Culture, symbols, rituals, and even political statements are all a part of the change process. Leadership occupies a similar theoretical vacuum: Leadership is treated as the management of small groups—the manager's implementation of strategies designed to improve group cohesion and productivity—but this is not leadership; in reality it is the attempt to disguise managerial functions by placing them under the rubric of leadership in the hope that workers will acquiesce to managerial directives. Leadership, I hope to demonstrate, is a much broader phenomenon. Organizational theories suffer the same fate, and these also need to be explored.

Thus, I believe that administrators and students of educational administration can make a difference. But they can only make this difference by adopting different ways of seeing; clearly, the orthodox perspective of educational administration is deficient. It needs to be infused with a critical view and an Ignatian vision. In an earlier work entitled *Educational Leadership: Leading with Mind and Heart,* we argue that possessing the knowledge and skills of leadership is only half of the battle. To be a complete leader, one must also develop a value system, or philosophy, of leadership that guides the leader's actions and provides the leader with the "human touch." It is through the lens of critical theory and the Ignatian vision that the "heart" of educational leadership is developed.

In this text I hope to acquaint the administrator and potential administrator with a different way of thinking about education and its administration. As a field of study, educational administration has come of age. The maturity of the field, however, requires its reconstruction as a moral and as a critical science. This theme is not as uncommon, as it once was. However, there is a huge disconnect between the knowledge of critical theory and the skills necessary to place it into actual practice. To this end, this text contains chapters that review the history of administrative theory, elaborate on the positivistic theory of administration, argue that administration needs to develop into a moral science, outline the Ignatian vision of leadership, explore the critical approach to leadership, integrate theory and practice, explore an organizational change process, and assess the effective implementation of positivism, critical theory, and the Ignatian vision. The final chapter contains a practical application of this approach to a case study involving the very controversial topic of education tuition vouchers.

CHAPTER 1

Educational Leadership

Effective leadership is offered as a solution to most of the problems of organizations everywhere. Schools will work, we are told, if principals and presidents provide strong instructional leadership. Around the world, administrators and managers say that their organizations would thrive if only senior management provided strategy, vision, and real leadership. Though the call for leadership is universal, there is much less clarity about what the term means.

In this chapter, we will argue the authenticity of the following definition of leadership:

> Leadership is the ability to establish and manage a creative climate open to change and continuous improvement where people are self-motivated toward the achievement of mutually developed goals in an environment of mutual trust and respect compatible with a mutually developed value system.

This definition assumes a positivist approach to educational administration that is informed by critical theory and the Ignatian vision. It defines leadership as a moral science, which is a postpositivist approach to understanding educational leadership, one that implies a positivist/functionalist approach informed by critical humanism and the Ignatian vision.

Leadership is an ability, which implies that it is both an inherent and a learned behavior, that is, both positivist and functionalist in nature. Managing and developing goals are also products of functionalism, as is creating a climate open to change. However, establishing a creative climate and establishing an environment of trust, along with developing a

5

value system implies the application of critical theory and the Ignatian vision. In order to add form to this vision of leadership, we begin by exploring the roots of educational leadership.

THE HISTORY OF LEADERSHIP

Historically, scholars in this field have searched for the one best leadership style that would be most effective at all times and in all instances. The notion that there could be one singular method of leading was precluded very early in the history of leadership study. Current thought is that there is no one best style. Rather, a combination of leadership styles, depending on the situation, has been found to be more appropriate and effective. To understand the evolution of leadership theory, we will take a historical approach and trace the progress of leadership theory beginning with the early theories that used the trait perspective and moving to the more current contingency theories of leadership

Trait theory suggests that one can evaluate leadership and propose ways of leading effectively by considering whether an individual possesses certain personality traits, social traits, and physical characteristics. Popular in the 1940s and 1950s, trait theory attempted to predict which individuals would successfully become leaders and, then, whether they would be successful. According to trait theorists, leaders differ from non-leaders in their drive, desire to lead, honesty and integrity, self-confidence, cognitive ability, and knowledge of the business that they are in.

Limitations in the ability of trait theory to predict effective leadership caused researchers during the 1950s to view a person's behavior, rather than personal traits, as a way of increasing leadership effectiveness. This view also paved the way for later situational theories.

The types of leadership behaviors investigated typically fell into two categories: production-oriented and employee-oriented. Production-oriented leadership involves acting primarily to get the task done. An administrator who tells his or her department chair to do whatever is necessary to develop a new curriculum in time for the start of the school year demonstrates production-oriented leadership. So does the administrator who uses an autocratic style or fails to involve workers in any aspect of decision making. On the contrary, employee-oriented leadership focuses on supporting the individual workers in their activities and involving the workers in decision making. A principal who demonstrates great concern for his or her teachers' satisfaction with their duties and commitment to their work has an employee-oriented leadership style.

Contingency or situational models differ from the earlier trait and behavioral models in asserting that no single way of leading works in all situations. Rather, appropriate behavior depends on the circumstances at a given time. Effective managers, they say, diagnose the situation, identify the leadership style that will be most effective, and then determine whether they can implement the required style. Early situational research suggested that subordinate, supervisor, and task considerations affect the appropriate leadership style in a given situation. The precise aspects of each dimension that influence the most effective leadership style vary. The idea that one can use leadership theory to predict whether a certain style will be effective is termed a positivist or functionalist approach to leadership.

Research suggests that the effect of leader behaviors on performance is altered by such intervening variables as the effort of subordinates, their ability to perform their jobs, the clarity of their job responsibilities, the organization of the work, the cooperation and cohesiveness of the group, the sufficiency of resources and support provided to the group, and the coordination of work group activities with those of other subunits. Thus, leaders must respond to these and broad cultural differences in choosing an appropriate style. A leader-environment-follower interaction theory of leadership notes that effective leaders first analyze deficiencies in the follower's ability, motivation, role perception, and work environment that inhibit performance and, then, act to eliminate these deficiencies.

Bolman and Deal have developed a unique situational leadership theory that analyzes leadership behavior through four frames of reference: structural, human-resource, political, and symbolic. Each of the frames offers a different perspective on what leadership is and how it operates in organizations. Each can result in either effective or ineffective conceptions of leadership.[1]

Structural leaders develop a new model of the relationship of structure, strategy, and environment for their organizations. They focus on implementation. The right answer helps only if it can be implemented. Structural leaders sometimes fail because they miscalculate the difficulty of putting their designs into place. They often underestimate the resistance that these plans will generate, and they take few steps to build a base of support for their innovations. In short, they are often undone by human-resource, political, and symbolic considerations. Structural leaders continually experiment, evaluate, and adapt, but because they fail to consider the entire environment in which they are situated, they are sometimes ineffective.

Human-resource leaders believe in people and communicate that belief. They are passionate about productivity through people. They demonstrate this faith in their words and actions and often build it into a philosophy, or credo, that is central to their vision of their organizations. Human-resource leaders are visible and accessible. Peters and Waterman popularized the notion of "management by wandering around," which posits that managers need to get out of their offices and interact with workers and customers. Many educational administrators have adopted this aspect of management.[2] For example, whenever we utilize Bolman and Deal's Frame Identification Survey, an overwhelming majority of my graduate students (teachers and administrators) identify with the human-resource frame of leadership.

In addition, effective human-resource leaders empower; that is, they increase participation, provide support, share information, and move decision making as far down the organization as possible. Human-resource leaders often like to refer to their employees as partners or colleagues. They want to make it clear that employees have a stake in the organization's success and a right to be involved in making decisions. When they are ineffective, however, they are seen as naive or weak.

Political leaders clarify what they want and what they can get. Political leaders are realists above all. They never let what they want cloud their judgment about what is possible. They assess the distribution of power and interests. The political leader needs to think carefully about the players, their interests, and their power; in other words, he or she must map the political terrain. Political leaders ask questions, such as whose support do I need? How do I go about getting it? Who are my opponents? How much power do they have? What can I do to reduce the opposition? Is the battle winnable? However, if ineffective, these leaders are perceived as being untrustworthy and manipulative.

The symbolic frame provides a fourth turn of the kaleidoscope of leadership. In this frame, the organization is seen as a stage, a theater in which every actor plays certain roles and attempts to communicate the right impressions to the right audiences. The main premise of this frame is that whenever reason and analysis fail to contain the dark forces of ambiguity, human beings erect symbols, myths, rituals, and ceremonies to bring order, meaning, and predictability out of chaos and confusion.

According to Bolman and Deal, symbolic, or transforming, leaders are visionary leaders, and visionary leadership is invariably symbolic. Examination of symbolic leaders reveals that they follow a consistent set of practices and rules. Transforming leaders use symbols to capture attention. When Diana Lam, for example, became principal of the Mackey Middle School in Boston in 1985, she knew that she faced a substantial challenge. Mackey had all the usual problems of urban public schools: decaying physical plant, lack of student discipline, racial tension, troubles with the teaching staff, low morale, and limited resources. The only good news was that the situation was so bad that almost any change would have been an improvement. In such a situation, symbolic leaders will try to do something visible, even dramatic, to let people know that changes are on the way. During the summer before she assumed her duties, Lam wrote a letter to every teacher to set up an individual meeting. She traveled to meet teachers wherever they wanted, driving two hours in one case. She asked teachers how they felt about the school and what changes they wanted.

Lam also felt that something needed to be done about the school building because nobody likes to work in a "dumpy" place. She decided that the front door and some of the worst classrooms had to be painted. She had few illusions about getting the bureaucracy of the Boston public schools to provide painters, so she persuaded some of her family members to help her do the painting. When school opened, students and staff members immediately saw that things were going to be different, if only symbolically. Perhaps even more importantly, staff members received a subtle challenge to make a contribution themselves.[3]

Each of these frames captures significant possibilities for leadership, but each is incomplete. In the early part of the century, leadership as a concept was rarely applied to management, and the implicit models of leadership were narrowly rational. In the 1960s and 1970s, human-resource leadership became fashionable. The literature on organizational leadership stressed openness, sensitivity, and participation. In recent years, symbolic leadership has moved to center stage, and the literature now offers advice on how to become a visionary leader with the power to transform organizational cultures. Organizations do need vision, but it is not their only need and not always their most important one. Leaders need to understand their own frame and its limits. Ideally, they will also learn to combine multiple frames into a more comprehensive and powerful style. It is only then that they will be able to personify my definition of leadership.

TRANSFORMATIONAL LEADERSHIP

Charismatic, or transformational, leaders use charisma to inspire their followers. They talk to them about how essential their performance is, how confident they are in their followers, how exceptional the followers are, and how they expect the group's performance to exceed expectations. Such leaders may use dominance, self-confidence, a need for influence, and a conviction of moral righteousness to increase their charisma and, consequently, their leadership effectiveness.

A transformational leader changes an organization by recognizing an opportunity and developing a vision, communicating that vision to organizational members, building trust in the vision, and achieving the vision by motivating organizational members. The leader helps subordinates recognize the need for revitalizing the organization by developing a felt need for change, overcoming resistance to change, and avoiding quick-fix solutions to problems. Encouraging subordinates to act as devil's advocates with regard to the leader, building networks outside the organization, visiting other organizations, and changing management processes to reward progress against competition also help them recognize a need for revitalization. Individuals must disengage from and disidentify with the past, as well as view change as a way of dealing with their disenchantments with the past or the status quo. The transformational leader creates a new vision and mobilizes commitment to it by planning or educating others. He or she builds trust through demonstrating personal expertise, self-confidence, and integrity. The charismatic leaders can also change the composition of the team, alter management processes, and help organizational members reframe the way they look at an organizational situation. The charismatic leaders must empower others to help achieve the vision. Finally, the transformational leaders must institutionalize the change by replacing old technical, political, cultural, and social networks with new ones.

For example, the leader can identify key individuals and groups, develop a plan for obtaining their commitment, and institute a monitoring system for following the changes. If an administrator wished to make an innovative program acceptable to the faculty and the school community, for example, he or she should follow the above plan and identify influential individuals who would agree to champion the new program, develop a plan to gain support from others in the community through personal contact or other means, and develop a monitoring system to assess the progress of the effort.

A transformational leader motivates subordinates to achieve beyond their original expectations by increasing their awareness of the importance of designated outcomes and ways of attaining them, by getting workers to see beyond their self-interest to that of the team, the school, the school system, and the larger society, by changing or expanding the individual's needs. Subordinates report that they work harder for such leaders. In addition, such leaders are judged to be higher in leadership potential by their subordinates as compared to the more common transactional leader.

One should be cognizant, however, of the negative side of charismatic leadership, which may exist if the leader overemphasizes devotion to him or herself, makes personal needs paramount, or uses highly effective communication skills to mislead or manipulate others. Such leaders may be so driven to achieve a vision that they ignore the costly implications of their goals. Nevertheless, recent research has verified the overall effectiveness of the transformational leadership style. I argue, however, that going beyond transformational leadership and, therefore, being even more effective would entail infusing it with the principles of critical theory and the Ignatian vision, which I will address more fully in future chapters.

NOTES

1. Lee B. Bolman and Terrance E. Deal, *Reframing Organizations* (San Francisco: Jossey Bass, 1991).

2. T. Peters and R. Waterman, *In Search of Excellence* (New York: Harper and Row, 1982).

3. E. Mark Hanson, *Educational Administration and Organizational Behavior* (Boston: Allyn and Bacon, 1991).

CHAPTER 2

The Positivist/Functionalist
Approach to Leadership

Administrative theorists in the twentieth century had an overriding concern for purging administration of any nonscientific dimensions. Administration as a field depended on a theoretical framework informed largely by a version of science derived from the tenants of logical positivism, a philosophical movement in the early part of the twentieth century. Logical positivism asserted that only scientific knowledge, which was verifiable in principle, was true knowledge and could be expressed in logical, and therefore true, form. This, of course, removed a good deal of human affairs from the realm of truth; values, ethics, and morality would simply become matters of assertion or preference. To its credit, logical positivism aimed at eliminating the mystic and metaphysical thought that concealed the structure of human relationships. At the same time though, it disallowed any scrutiny of questions of human values, declaring these to be scientifically meaningless and, thus, illegitimate concerns for consideration. In this way of thinking, value statements are incapable of scientific proof; therefore, they do not have any meaning within a scientific system. The only system that could provide true, verifiable knowledge was science.

Administrative theory was built on this foundation, and it remains the dominant way of approaching administration even today. Over the years our institutions have built a structure of administrative training programs that has uncritically accepted the assumptions about people and ideas generated by logical positivism. As a result, the practice of administration is sometimes divorced from theoretical reflection on the most vital and dynamic parts of the field—its moral, ethical, and value-based dimensions. This position is aided and abetted by the strict interpretation of the First Amendment's separation of church and state provisos. The skills one associates with administration are themselves based on such evaluative approaches to the world. Strong empirical work should be valued, but within the context established by an understanding of the nature of the social and educational system of which we are a part. Administration is not just a technical skill: It is a way of ordering the world according to a set of values and beliefs. Administration exists within various contexts: the managerial context, concerned with the distribution and acquisition of resources; the leadership context, concerned with the development and change of the institution and of the people within it; and the sociocultural context, concerned with the nature of administration and the institution within our social and cultural systems. This last context has frequently been neglected in studies of the administration of education, yet is crucial for a proper understanding of the total administrative task. This is why, in and of itself, the positivistic approach will not provide a leader with the philosophical base needed to bring one to administrative self-actualization.

Going hand in glove with the positivist approach is functionalist theory. Functionalism, which has been the prevailing theoretical framework in the social sciences throughout the twentieth century, argues that society operates like the human body: Like living organisms, all societies possess basic functions that they must carry out to survive. Like living organisms, they evolve structures to carry out these functions. For example, the human body is composed of many interdependent organs, each of which carries out a vital function. Every organ must be healthy, and all must work together to maintain the health of the entire body. If any organ malfunctions, the entire body may die. Similarly, societies, in order to survive, develop specialized structures to carry out vital functions as they reproduce themselves, recruit or produce new members, distribute goods and services, and allocate power.

One of the most important functions is that of transmission. In the traditional functionalist view of social transmission, each elder generation passes on to each succeeding generation the rules, customs, and appropriate behaviors for operation in the society. They do so through the principal socializing institutions or transmitters of the culture, such as families, churches, and schools. By participating in these institutions, individuals accept their roles within the social structure of society. Functionalists identify not only the various functions within a society, but also the connections between the components of a societal system and the relations between different systems. For example, functionalists assert that if one socializing institution is not fulfilling its function, another will take over its role to maintain the equilibrium of the society. In today's society, functionalists would argue that as in more families, both parents work, schools have taken over many of the functions formerly performed by the family.

Functional analysis has become an inescapable part of the training and world view of most educational scholars. Although they may not accept all of the tenets of traditional functional social theory, all educational scholars use its categories as basic analytic tools to describe social systems. However, functionalism has been criticized, both because it rejects conflict and change as viable, and often valuable, social processes, and because its proponents have asserted that it is the only approach that produces objective, unbiased, or truly scientific findings.[1] Functionalists may do this because their training has never presented alternative perspectives, and also because they are so steeped in the functional-analysis approach that it appears to be the truth, rather than merely one way of looking at the world. However, other theories are available, some of them variations of functionalism, and these may provide more adequate or critical explanations.

STRUCTURAL FUNCTIONALISM

An important variant of functionalism is structural functionalism. Structuralists assume that human systems have an underlying, but unobservable, coherence based upon formal rules, signs, and arrangements. Structuralists seek to understand human phenomena, such as systems of meaning, language, and culture, by identifying these underlying structures and making inferences about the underlying social structure based upon patterns observed in human life.

Central to structural functionalism is the conviction that the structures in a social system must maintain equilibrium with each other to sustain societal health. Conflict, like an illness, is an aberration that the healthy system avoids and seeks to resolve as quickly as possible. Any change takes place only gradually in healthy systems because it constitutes a disruption of normalcy. Revolutions and other forms of rapid change are signs of illness. Many structural functionalists believe that any social structure found in a system must have some function and probably serves some crucial need, even if that need is not immediately apparent. Some social scientists have used this argument to oppose change in general, especially in traditional societies, on the grounds that even practices that seem morally offensive, such as the cremation of Hindu widows upon the death of their spouses, must have utility within the given culture. They hold that to remove such structures might cause harm to the system and should, like surgery to the human body, be undertaken only with great care and in extreme circumstances. However, critics of functionalism contend that it ignores the notion, integral to critical theories, that conflict and contradictions are inherent in a social system and, in fact, stimulate its adaptation to new conditions.

FUNCTIONALISM AND SCHOOLING

Functionalists view educational systems as one of the structures that carry out the function of transmitting attitudes, values, skills, and norms from one generation to another. Sociologists, such as Dreeden, Durkheim, and Merton, have described this process.[2] According to functionalists, educational systems perpetuate the accepted culture. The concept of accepted culture implies that there is consensus on which values, attitudes, and behaviors should be transmitted. When conflict over values does occur, adjustments are made to regain consensus and keep the system balanced. For example, in mid-twentieth-century America, conflict arose over whether school curricula should portray America as a white-dominated society into which immigrants were expected to assimilate or as a multicultural society in which differences were celebrated. The past several decades have witnessed a variety of adaptations in curricula, a reflection of attempts to arrive at a new consensus.

Functionalists believe that schooling serves to reinforce the existing social and political order. Because they assume there is consensus on how power is used and to whom it is allocated, they therefore view the social system as benign and accept existing class structures as appropriate. Because their perspective constitutes the current conventional wisdom about schools, the descriptions on the next few pages will seem quite familiar. We will soon examine other theories, however, and will see how interpretations of the purposes of schooling change when looked at through different theoretical lenses. Regardless of their particular orientation though, theorists do not necessarily disagree with the functional description of how schools are organized; rather, they disagree on the functions schools are said to have in society. They also differ in what they believe to be the desired goals or purposes of schooling.

The purposes attributed to schools fall into four general categories: intellectual, political, economic, and social. The three primary intellectual purposes of schooling are acquisition of the following:

1. Cognitive skills
2. Substantive knowledge
3. Inquiry skills

The common response to questions as to why children are sent to school is to learn. They are expected to acquire the knowledge and skills outlined above. In 1988 U.S. Secretary of Education stated, "American parents want their schools to do one thing above all others: teach their children to read, write, and speak well." This view has changed little in the intervening years. Businesses and industry also view schools as institutions whose job it is to impart both cognitive skills and a body of substantive knowledge in the natural and social sciences. The recent outcry around high-school students' lack of knowledge has been over alleged inattention to the purpose of education. The response has been to implement standards-based education.

Schools also are viewed as places that must produce future citizens and workers. To that end, they serve four major political purposes:

1. To educate future citizens for appropriate participation in the given political order
2. To promote patriotism by teaching myths, history, and stories about the country, its leaders, and its government
3. To promote the assimilation of immigrants
4. To ensure order, public civility, and conformity to laws

Functionalists believe that schooling facilitates knowledge about and integration into the political system. It is a means by which common social and political values are transmitted to young people and others, like immigrants, who initially may not share them. This goal has been one of the most important of modern public schooling.

Early American leaders believed that republican forms of government were required to educate citizens so they could participate wisely in the political system—vote, run for public office, and make informed decisions about government. Hence, they believed publicly financed schools should be provided for all—at least for all white males.

One of the earliest plans for providing free elementary education to both males and females was introduced to the Virginia legislature in 1779 by Thomas Jefferson. In his "Bill for the More General Diffusion of Knowledge," Jefferson proposed that public elementary schools be established in each county so that all children would receive three years of reading, writing, and computation. The most talented boys would then go on for a partly free education in regional grammar schools. A final selection for the most talented boy from all the schools would then attend the College of William and Mary at public expense.

Jefferson's plan, unlike those in the New England and other colonies, envisioned an articulated system of schools from elementary school to college. This articulated system sought to link requirements from each lower level to prerequisites in each higher one and to elevate a few males from the lower classes to the ranks of potential leaders. However, the plan did not explicitly teach citizenship. It emphasized a classical curriculum of Greek, Latin, English, Geography, Arthmetic, and American History, rather than government or civics. Jefferson believed that literacy and a free press were sufficient for making wise political decisions.

Jefferson's plan provided no equal opportunities for women or minorities, and it was never enacted. However, it did formalize the idea that schools were critical to the development of leadership in a democracy. This type of thinking continues to inform the way many people view schools today.

Horace Mann, often called the father of American education, believed that schools should not only produce leaders, but also train citizens. Foreshadowing John Dewey and others, Mann felt that a national political consensus could be developed through the teaching of common values and beliefs in public schools. During Mann's tenure as Secretary of the Massachusetts Board of Education (1837–1848), political tension, mass immigration, and class conflict were causing great concern. Mann was active in school reform; as editor of the *Common School Journal*, he advocated the establishment of publicly supported elementary schools, open to children of all socioeconomic classes, to provide basic literacy and to instill social and political values for a unified American identity. Such a common school would be the key to reforming society and creating a more stable union. His plan was supported by leaders of the dominant culture—industrialists, church leaders, and the business community—who felt that instilling respect for a common order would build a productive and complacent work force.

At the end of the nineteenth century, the influx of immigrants from southern and eastern Europe prompted educators' efforts to assimilate newcomers. Americanization programs were established to teach language, customs, and laws. Especially after World War I, schools were used not only to Americanize immigrants, but also to stimulate patriotism in all children. Reciting the Pledge of Allegiance and singing patriotic songs in school were viewed as training for later allegiance and service to the nation. Participation in student government and competitive sports were encouraged in order to develop school spirit, which later would be transferred to the country. Current curricular trends differ little from those described above. High schools require civics and economics with special emphasis on the free-enterprise system; children still learn political history and myths, and they still recite the Pledge of Allegiance; and political education and English-as-a-second-language classes are required for recent immigrants.

According to functionalists, schooling serves two major economic purposes:

1. To prepare students for later work roles
2. To select and train the labor forces

Functionalists believe that schools prepare students for the work force, in part, by teaching attitudes, technical skills, and social behavior appropriate to the work place, such as cooperation, conformity to authority, punctuality, gender-appropriate attitudes, neatness, task orientation, care of property, and allegiance to the team. Schools also act as "sorting machines," categorizing students by academic ability and, then, pointing them toward appropriate career goals. In this way, schools create a meritocracy, a hierarchical social structure organized by ability, and they distribute individuals to fill the diverse roles required by a complex industrial work force. Such a meritocracy assumes that no major external impediments stand in the way of success for able, hard-working individuals.

Schools' stratification of students and creation of an ability-based hierarchical ranking serves to link occupational to social-class differences in society. As the United States industrialized near the turn of the nineteenth century, the concepts of human capital and manpower planning came to dominate educational thinking. The human-capital school of thought, which originated in the late 1950s, calculates the rate of return from investing in schooling; it is measured by lifetime earnings minus the costs of education, including opportunity costs, or the amount of money not earned while in school. Humans are viewed as economic resources, and their laboring ability is likened to physical capital, such as money, coal, steel, or electrical power. Just as physical capital can grow by being invested wisely, the value of human capital can be increased by investing in, or acquiring more, education.[3]

Human-capital theorists thus view young people as commodities in the labor market and schools as the means of increasing the capacity of these resources by increasing their skills and knowledge. By supporting public education, turn-of-the-century industrialists invested in human resources just as they invested in physical capital and other kinds of resources. They also trained selected students for the work force. Industrial growth was believed to be intimately linked to a nation's ability to increase its supply of skilled human capital. School-business partnerships, such as the "Adopt a School" program, whereby local businesses invest in schools, are current examples of the belief in human capital. This belief has been one of the strongest catalysts to the growth of educational systems in developing countries.

Finally, functionalists believe that schools serve three major social purposes:

1. To promote a sense of social and moral responsibility
2. To serve as sites for the solution or amelioration of social problems

3. To supplement the efforts of other institutions of socialization, such as the family and the church

In traditional societies, the family, church, and community transmitted social and moral values to youth for the maintenance of culture. As nations became more complex, children did not always follow the paths of their parents. More complex skills were needed for work, and schools were called upon more and more to assist in the training and socialization of children. Since the nineteenth century, schools have been viewed also as the primary institution for solving social problems. In fact, in the 1890s the sociologist Edward Ross argued that the school had replaced the church and family as the primary instiller of social values, and he described education as in inexpensive alternative to the police.[4]

In the twentieth century, social goals have become a very real and vital component of schooling. Schools have been called upon to solve such problems as juvenile delinquency, poverty, child abuse, drug addiction, teenage pregnancy, sexually transmitted diseases, and lack of highway safety. Social services have been incorporated into schools on the grounds that well-fed, rested, and healthy children learn more readily and are less likely to drop out. They also are supported by the belief that children are more easily influenced by reform movements than are adults. Service programs also facilitate American egalitarian notions of equal opportunity and fair play.

FUNCTIONALISM AND LEADERSHIP

The principles of functionalism and positivism enunciated above also impact this theories' view of administration and leadership. Current debate in administrative theory in education centers around two different approaches to the study and practice of administration: the functionalist perspective and the critical mode. Functionalism in administration is represented by what might be called orthodox or mainstream theory. Taking its legacy from Taylorism, human relations, and systems theory, the research within this frame tends to be positivistic, objectivistic, and supposedly neutral. The majority of the theoretical and research-based work done in educational administration reflects a functionalist frame of mind. Griffiths, for example, reviews certain prominent researchers in educational administration and finds, "Both the past and present researchers can be said to be working within structural-functionalist theory. Aside from being less rigorous at present, there is really little difference between the two sets in the nature of the theory they espouse."[5] In general, mainstream theorists in educational administration espouse quantitative research that explores categories of behavior derived from structural-functional analyses of school organizations. The literature is rife with studies of communication patterns, role structures, school climate, motivation patterns, and so on. All of these studies assume that organizations are concrete entities populated by role players and that systematic study of these entities will yield reliable and predictable knowledge. Science, not philosophy, governs in the hope that a critical mass of empirical studies will eventually result in the accumulation of a verified, or at least not falsified, body of knowledge that will rationalize practice: "When theory is based on systems that are logical, rational, explicit, and quantitative, practice will be similarly rational."[6] The prevalent assumption is that current practice is clouded by values and emotions and is simply more or less nonrational. It is this way of thinking that spawned transformational leadership. Critics of functionalism would cynically reflect that practitioners need a science of administration based in functionalism to rescue them from their own humanity. While this assessment of functionalism in administration is harsh, a number of the leading scholars in the field, challenged by alternative viewpoints, are indeed rethinking their positions. Sometimes this results in paradigm shifts; at other times, in a vigorous defense of functionalist methods. An alternative approach, which has resulted in controversy in the field, is critical theory. Critical theory offers a new frame for educational administrators and theoreticians to consider.

NOTES

1. Peter Gronn and Peter Ribbins, "Leaders in Context: Postpositivist Approaches To Understanding Educational Leadership," *Educational Administration Quarterly* 32(3) (August 1996): 452–473.

2. Robert Merton, *Social Theory and Social Structure* (New York: The Free Press, 1957).

3. M. S. Archer, *Culture and Agency: The Place of Culture in Social Theory* (Cambridge: Cambridge University Press, 1988).

4. E. Ross, R. R. Ross, and M. G. Ross, *Relating and Interacting* (Englewood Cliffs, NJ: Prentice Hall, 1982).

5. D. Griffiths and Peter Ribbins, Leadership Matters in Education: Regarding Secondary Headship (1995) Inaugural lecture, University of Birmingham, Edgbaston.

6. Wayne Hoy and Cecil Miskel, *Educational Administration Theory, Research and Practice*, 6th ed. (Boston: McGraw-Hill, 1982).

CHAPTER 3

Critical Theory and Leadership

The term critical theory derives from the critique of previous theories that seek to explain how the social world operates and is organized. Critical theory does not involve mere fault-finding; rather, it requires unearthing or deconstructing hidden assumptions that govern society, with emphasis on the legitimacy of power relationships and deconstructing their claims to authority. It examines the current structure of society in which dominant socioeconomic groups exploit and oppress subordinate groups. Critical theorists refer to active involvement by participants as human agency and believe that despite the influence of oppressive reproductive forces, hope for transformation of society is maintained because of the existence of this agency.[1]

Historically, critical theory has its roots in a variety of traditional theories. First, it combines both macro and micro analyses of social phenomena. It uses the analytic basis and many of the concepts of both functionalism and conflict theory. It shares with conflict theory a concern about social and economic inequality and a conviction that inequality is determined by the economic structure, especially the ownership of property. Like conflict theorists, critical theorists believe that contradictions are inherent in social organizations, or are simultaneously held or acted upon in them, but that mutually opposing beliefs and practices act as destabilizing agents to force change. Often contradictions can be found between social myths and beliefs and actual social behavior. For example, Americans' belief in equality is contradicted by the simultaneous practice of tracking students according to ability. Critical theorists believe that contradictions are points of leverage within oppressive systems. As individuals learn to identify the contradictions that affect their lives, they also can become aware of the forces that oppress them. With growth in awareness, they can begin to transform their lives.

Critical pedagogues believe that social reality is constructed and operates at multiple levels of meaning. However, they consider knowledge and understanding of meaning to be a source of inequality insofar as they are distributed unequally by race, class, gender, and other ascribed characteristics. For example, they have called attention to gender and social-class differences in the way high-school counselors give different career advice to males and females and to high- and low-income students. In their research, critical theorists ask the following questions: What are the sources of inequality and oppression in society? How do individuals experience life in social organizations? How can individuals achieve autonomy in the face of societal oppression? How are language and communication patterns used to oppress people? And, how do people construct positive and negative identities?

HISTORICAL ROOTS OF CRITICAL THEORY

The critical pedagogy perspective grows out of strongly held beliefs that schooling cannot be separated from the social context within which it takes place. Thus, a discourse on ethics, the distribution of power, and the plight of the underserved must be included in any debate on how education should be delivered. The critical view emanated from the post–World War I belief that however terrible the conflict might be, it was necessary to clean the slate of social, political, and economic evils. These theorists believed that the insights and methodological skills of social scientists could be used to create a new millennium. However, by the 1930s, the rise of Nazism, the Great Depression, and the demise of the Weimar Republic made it apparent that World War I had not set the stage for Utopian developments. Neither war nor the new natural and social sciences had solved age-old problems, and the world was on the verge of another horrible war. The despair over these conditions destroyed the conviction that the sciences could solve human problems, a conviction that had persisted since the eighteenth-century Enlightenment. Scientists were left believing that existing social-science theory and methods were faulty and in need of radical critique or wholesale elimination.

Some of the principal critics of contemporary theory are discussed in the following sections. We provide only a brief glimpse at the works of these theorists and how their work has affected educational thought.

The Frankfurt School

The Frankfurt School refers to a group of social theorists and philosophers who worked in Germany at the Institute for Social Research (1923–1960), which was connected to the University of Frankfurt. Max Horkheimer was the director of the Institute from 1931 until he retired in 1958. He coined the term critical theory to contrast what he and his colleagues were doing with the positivism of Descartes and Saint Simon.[2] Among the best-known of these theorists were Theodor Adorno, Herbert Marcuse, Erich Fromm, and Walter Benjamin. Members of the Frankfurt School, many of whom were Jewish, relocated the Institute to Columbia University in New York during World War II because of Nazi persecution, returning to Frankfurt in 1949. Its members' participation in American academic life, where they conducted a number of landmark empirical studies of race and prejudice, influenced generations of American scholars. Their critical perspectives are the foundation for critical theory today.

Much like the current work in critical theory, what emerged from their work was no single shared theory, but rather a perspective with several common elements. The analysis of the Frankfurt School was a critique of traditional or bourgeois perspectives, which had assumed that social phenomena could be understood through scientific methods of description, classification, generalization, and quantification. This traditional view, referred to as positivism, is patterned after that used in the natural sciences. Knowledge gained by means of this type of research was represented as objective, value-free, and scientific.

Frankfurt School theorists were critical of the positivistic model on the grounds that human phenomena could not be understood in the same way that physical phenomena could. Whereas positivistic research tends to ignore historical antecedents, critical theorists consider historical analysis central to an understanding of social phenomena. The Frankfurt School members believed that neither social phenomena nor research methods—and even the decision to use specific methods—could be separated from their social and historical context. Both were embedded in social values and, therefore, could not be considered objective. Rather, they were expressive of a particular theoretical or philosophical position. Critical theorists advocate recognition of subjectivity through a process of self-criticism and self-reflection; they assert that no research is truly objective or value-free.

The Frankfurt School was critical of the economic determinism of Marxism because the latter ignored the influence of culture in the perpetuation of inequality and oppression. However, they shared with Marxists, a concern for injustice, oppression, and inequality and looked toward the radical transformation of social arrangements in order to increase human freedom.

Antonio Gramsci

Gramsci was an Italian Marxist, both a theorist and an activist, who is best known for his *Selections from the Prison Notebooks*, which he wrote during eleven years of imprisonment for political activities during the 1930s, and which was translated into English in 1971. One of his most important contributions was his notion of the individual as an active, rather than a passive, agent, even in the face of extremely oppressive conditions. Gramsci was particularly concerned with the struggles of working-class men and women in Italy and the ways in which the dominant ideology of the state shapes individual consciousness. He used the term hegemony to describe the process by which the worldview of the dominant state maintains control through the socializing activity of institutions. Gramsci argued that social change could occur only when revolutionary consensus, for which intellectuals provided a catalyst, was fully achieved among subordinate classes. However, once that occurred, alternative institutions could be created which would change the hegemony of the dominant groups. An example might be a group of female elementary teachers who resist the oppression of a male-dominated administrative structure by working together toward a structure in which they share in the governance of the school.

Jurgen Habermas and Michel Foucault

Two other theorists who have contributed significantly to contemporary critical theory in education are Jurgen Habermas and Michel Foucault. Both were concerned with the relationship between knowledge and power. These theorists believed that knowledge is as important a social resource as land, money, or legal position. Those who control access to knowledge also control access to the power structure. Further, Foucault asserted that power is knowledge, in that what is taken to be real or true knowledge is defined as such by powerful groups in society. Real knowledge, then, is what people in power—professional societies, scientific bodies, the government, leading cultural groups— declare to be true and establish as standards.

Habermas examined how restrictions on the flow of information contribute to inequality in society. He argued that valid knowledge derives only from open, free, and uninterrupted dialogue. Not even science is exempt from this dialogue. Habermas rejected the idea of an authoritative, neutral, apolitical science, as well as the possibility of separating facts and values because each is a product of social and historical context. Foucault also suggested that knowledge or truth is never free from the effects of history, power, and entrenched interests:

> Truth is a thing of this world: it is produced only by virtue of multiple forms of constraint. And it induces regular effects of power. Each society has its regime of truth, its "general politics" of truth: that is, the types of discourse which it accepts and makes function as true; the mechanisms and instances which enable one to distinguish true and false statements, the means by which each is sanctioned; the techniques and procedure accorded value in the acquisition of truth; the status of those who are charged with saying what counts as true.[3]

Paulo Freire

Freire was a Brazilian educator whose work translates the notions of agency and power into strategies useful for educators. Freire spent his life working with students and educators to challenge the constraints and inequities of traditional institutions. He drew on the radical Catholicism of Liberation theology, which emphasizes the role of individuals in understanding and creating their own salvation, free from the mediation or definition of Church authority. Liberation theologians taught literacy skills to peasants by having teachers and students engage in dialogue over texts that were meaningful to them in their daily lives. Learning to read and talk about the conditions in which they lived gave peasants the courage to speak up against powerful agencies, such as the government, the police, and the Church. Speaking up, in turn, led to efforts to transform the conditions of their lives.

One of Freire's central beliefs was that teachers must respect their students' cultures by providing opportunities for them to participate in their own learning. Teachers and students also must be self-reflective in discovering the ways in which state hegemony has structured their experiences. Freire viewed teachers and students as active agents in understanding, criticizing, resisting, and transforming schooling practices that serve to maintain a society that oppresses large groups of people. In the United States, Freire's ideas have been used widely in literacy programs in and out of classrooms. They have tended to lose the social revolutionary vigor which they possess in Latin America, where Freire's followers have challenged the oppressive practices of the Catholic Church, the military, the government, and large landowners.

CRITICAL THEORY AND AMERICAN EDUCATION

The assumption that schools are the sites of power struggles between dominant and subordinate groups is a given for critical theorists. A major theme in their research is the analysis of how schools are used to help dominant groups maintain their position of power, as well as how subordinate groups resist this domination. On the macrostructural level, critical theorists view schools as places where a class-based society is reproduced through the use of the economic, cultural, and hegemonic capital of the dominant social class. Henry Giroux, currently one of the leading critical theorists, writes, "Reproduction refers here to texts (language and communication patterns) and social practices whose message, inscribed within specific historical settings and social contexts, function primarily to legitimate the interests of the dominant social order. I want to argue that these can be characterized as texts, as social practices about pedagogy, and refer primarily to categories of meaning constructed so as to legitimize and reproduce interests expressed in dominant ideologies."[4]

Informed by conflict theorists, critical theorists contend that the power of dominant groups is reinforced within schools. By means of academic selection, socioeconomic stratification, and government regulation of curricular and pedagogical modes, dominant, white, male, and middle- or upper-class cultural standards are imposed on children. One can see, therefore, why the critical pedagogues often find functionalist theory to be repugnant, in that its research often reinforces these "injustices."

Critical theorists view classrooms as sites of cultural production, where people interact to construct meaning. Issues of power and control are worked out in classrooms by individuals. If those involved in the schooling process are able to resist the oppressive practices of schooling, and if critical consciousness can be developed by teachers, administrators, and students, schools can become sites of social change, rather than of social reproduction. In effect, what they are arguing is to do just that. If educational administrators can be sensitized to the need to inform their functionalistic perspective with the principles of critical theory and the Ignatian vision, they will have led their communities to become sites of social change, rather than social reproduction.

Therefore, critical theorists believe that their task is to uncover the ways in which dominant ideology is translated into practice in schools and the ways in which human agency mutes the impact of that ideology. Thus, critical educational theorists are deeply concerned with the art and practice of teaching. They argue that teachers must become "transformative intellectuals" and "critical pedagogues" in order to resist the oppression of the dominant ideology and to produce a liberating culture within schools. In other words, teachers must continue to be active, questioning learners. They must have knowledge, as well as critical ability, so they can question not only their own practice, but school structure as well. Students also must be taught to become active, critical, and engaged learners in a stimulating environment.

CRITICAL THEORY AND THE PURPOSES OF SCHOOLING

Critical theorists and functionalists would agree that the purpose of schooling would be to reproduce the dominant culture. But criticalists offer a way out. Critical theorists emphasize the power of individuals to structure their own destinies and to ameliorate the oppressive nature of the institutions in which they live. In many ways, the focus that critical theorists place on the liberating qualities of critical thinking resemble that of John Dewey and other educational philosophers who felt that an educated citizenry would facilitate the preservation of a democratic and egalitarian society. However, critical theorists have been faulted for failing to put their theory into practice. Much of their work consists of theoretical writing, and much of that is written in obscure language unintelligible to the very teachers and students whom they hope to emancipate.

The critical pedagogy perspective grows out of a strongly held belief that schooling cannot be separated from the social context within which it takes place. Thus, a discourse on ethics, the distribution of power, and the plight of the underserved must be included in any debate on how education should be delivered. Believers in critical pedagogy decry the current emphasis on testing to assess academic achievement, asserting that testing alone is not really authentic assessment. Personal narrative which expresses one's cultural, intellectual, and social background and experience is an essential component of authentic assessment.

CRITICAL THEORY AND EDUCATIONAL ADMINISTRATION

Functionalism has been challenged by perspectives informed by the critical work of social thinkers from Britain, Germany, and France, as well as the United States. When applied to schools and administration, this work has been labeled as the critical theory of educational administration. It can be discussed in terms of theoretical reflections and practical implications.

The theoretical basis involves a critique of positivism and the related ideas of fact-value separation and value neutrality in administration, a critique of modern rationality as it is embodied in administrative principle, and a focus on the ideas of power and liberation as concerns for administration. The fact-value distinction arises out of the positivist assertion that only facts constitute legitimate scientific knowledge. Scientific knowledge, in this view, is that which can be reduced to "true" statements, statements that correspond to mathematical logic. Because values do not lend themselves to this kind of reduction, they lie outside the ken of science and are meaningless for the scientist. A science of administration based on these principles cannot consider the value dimension except as it is recorded as a series of facts; for example, a percentage of the population believes in x. The administrator's role then is not to make a right or good or wise decision (value-based), but to make an efficient decision (fact-based) that achieves some goal set by others. Critical theory in administration argues that, first, this presents a too-constricted view of the scientific enterprise, and second, that the fact-value dichotomy is artificial and false. Facts are identified as facts only through our values; in making any kind of decision, the administrator is advancing someone's values. Every decision about what "is" the case is also a statement about what "ought" to be the case. A decision to close a school, for example, may be an expression of the hard-headed fact that the school system needs to save resources, but it is also a statement of values and of priorities: This school, and not some other school, ought to be closed because no other option is as viable.

Critical theory has another concern in that conventional wisdom says that administrators are the only means to achieve predetermined ends. Instrumental rationality means that rationality is largely considered a function of means-ends chains: An action is rational if it achieves some end. Rational actions are therefore instrumental, but if all actions are treated this way, what becomes of the search for the ends themselves? Formal or substantive rationality is concerned with searching for desired, valued ends of a substantive and political nature. In administrative thought in particular, and in society in general, the substantive questions are not questions at all—they are givens. Citizens have limited input into how the system is conducted, in terms of such issues as distribution of wealth and the development of policy. Administration serves as a means for implementing policies established by elite decision makers and demanded by technological imperatives, rather than as a guide for involving all citizens in the democratic determination of ends.

In administrative theory, rationality becomes a property of organizations and organizational systems rather than of individuals. Rationality is only considered in its instrumental sense, as a means for achieving ends. Because individuals do not have the capacity to consider all alternative means for achieving those ends, they are "boundedly rational" (Simon), they are not fully rational.[5] The organization, which comprises groups of individuals, is rational because it can draw on the rationalities of many individuals. Each alone is limited, but when organized, these individuals complement each other; thus, the organization as a unit is more rational than any given individual in it. This delegation of rationality to the organization is uncomfortable for a critical theory of administration. It displaces responsibility for rational action from the individual to the organization; the person thereby loses the ability to make decisions concerning ends and means.

We can see from this discussion that organizational or societal ends or goals are of major importance to the development of a critical frame. Which ends to pursue, whom they benefit and whom they harm, and how they contribute to a social vision are crucial questions in this approach. This means a commitment to the idea of praxis. An administrative and other social theory must go beyond mere analysis of institutional structures to show how theory can inform action, and action can lead to justice. Praxis, though, is not just given: It is dialectical in that it is continually and critically challenged, reformulated, and challenged again. Thus, a critical theory can also be a practical theory.

Another concern of critical theory is communicative practices. Rational and free discourse is a hallmark of democratic society, but authoritarian and bureaucratic structures often impede such expression. Lines of authority and unequal status differentials restrict communication and distort issues of a public nature. Finally, cultural concerns also become part of a critical frame of administration. School organizations have cultures, and cultures include shared sagas, myths, rituals, and symbols. Cultures also serve to rationalize and legitimize administrative actions and, thus, can transmit a hierarchy of power and domination within the school. Administrators from a critical frame will be particularly sensitive to this issue. The critical theory of administration is based largely on the work of the Frankfurt School. For administrators, this perspective parallels what will be discussed later as the humanist approach. Although basically sympathetic to the interpretive approach of Greenleaf (Servant Leadership) and others, critical theory attempts to go further by analyzing how constructed social structures themselves become seen as real and, so, solidify the way power is distributed in a society. Such a theory is concerned with analysis and education, with exposing so-called objective conditions and helping to show future possibilities.[6]

The two frameworks of functionalism and critical theory offer different ways of conceptualizing organization and administration. One aims at discovering regularities, leading to prediction and lawlike regularization of administration; the other looks at how meanings are created and choices imposed. A critical theory has a threefold purpose: (1) to develop empirically based, nonpositivistic studies of organization and administration; (2) to engage in the interpretation of meaning; and (3) to evaluate the potential of social structures to empower or disempower the individuals within them. These three are termed the empirical, hermeneutic, and emancipatory interests of a critical theory. The practical implications of these interests will be discussed later.

NOTES

1. William Foster, *Paradigms and Promises* (New York: Prometheus Books, 1986).

2. Kathleen Bennett de Marrais and Margaret D. Le Compte, *The Way Schools Work*, 3rd ed. (New York: Addison-Wesley, 1995).

3. Michel Foucault, *Power/Knowledge* (New York: Pantheon Books, 1980).

4. Henry Giroux, "Theories of Reproduction and Resistance in the New Sociology of Education," *Harvard Educational Review* 53 (1983): 257–293.

5. J. G. March and H. A. Simon, *Organizations* (New York: John Wiley, 1958).

6. Max De Pree, *Leadership Is an Art* (New York: Dell Publishing, 1989).

CHAPTER 4

Educational Administration
as a Moral Science

In this chapter we address how an educational administrator should be educated and trained for such a position. Traditionally, there has been only one answer: Practicing and future administrators should study educational administration in order to learn the scientific basis for decision making and to understand the scientific research that underlies proper administration. Universities train future administrators with texts that stress the scientific research done on administrative behavior, review various studies of teacher and student performance, and provide a few techniques for accomplishing educational goals. Such approaches instill a reverence for the scientific method, but an unfortunate disregard for any humanistic and critical development of the art of administration.

We are suggesting a different approach. Although there is certainly an important place for scientific research in backing empirically supported administrative behavior, we suggest that educational administrators also be critical humanists. Humanists appreciate the usual and unusual events of our lives and engage in an effort to develop, challenge, and liberate human souls. They are critical because they are educators and, therefore, are not satisfied with the status quo; rather, they hope to change individuals and institutions for the better and to improve social conditions for all. I will argue that an administrative science be reconstructed as a moral science. An administrative science can be empirical, but it must also incorporate hermeneutic (the science of interpreting and understanding others) and critical dimensions. Social science has increasingly recognized that it must be informed by moral questions. The paradigm of natural science does not always apply when dealing with human issues. As a moral science, the science of administration is concerned with the resolution of moral dilemmas. A critical and a literary model of administration helps to provide us with the necessary context and understanding wherein such dilemmas can be wisely resolved, and we can truly actualize our potential as administrators and leaders.

One's tendency toward critical humanism often depends on one's philosophy of how human beings behave in the workplace. The two extremes of the continuum might be described as those leaders who believe that human beings are basically lazy and will do the very least that they need to do to get by in the workplace, and those who believe that people are basically industrious and, if given the choice, would opt for doing the "right thing." I believe that today's most effective leaders hold the latter view. I agree with Max De Pree, owner and CEO of the highly successful Herman Miller Furniture Company. In his book *Leadership Is an Art*, De Pree argues that a leader's function is to "liberate people to do what is required of them in the most effective and humane way possible."[1] Instead of catching people doing something wrong, our goal as enlightened leaders is to catch them doing something right. Such behavior is reflective of a leader who is in the humanist, if not also in the critical, tradition.

THE HUMANIST TRADITION

The first responsibility of a leader is to define reality through a vision. The last is to say thank you. In between, the leader must become the servant of the servants. Being a leader means having the opportunity to make a meaningful difference in the lives of those who allow leaders to lead. This approach summarizes what it means to be an administrator and leader in the humanist tradition.

Whether one is a successful leader can be determined by looking at one's followers. Are they reaching their potentials? Are they learning? Are they able to change without bitterness? Are they able to achieve the institution's goals and objectives? Can they manage conflict among themselves? Do they have an internal locus of control? Are they concerned with the social implications of educational policy? Where the answer to these questions is an emphatic yes, an effective and humanist leader resides.

I prefer to think about administration in terms of what the Gospel writer Luke calls the "one who serves." The leader owes something to the institution he or she leads. The leader is seen in this context as steward, rather than owner or proprietor. Administration as a moral science requires the leader to think about his or her stewardship in terms of legacy, values, direction, and effectiveness.

Too many of today's administrators are interested only in immediate results that bolster their career goals. Long-range goals are left to their successors. I believe that this approach fosters autocratic leadership, which often produces short-term results, but militates against creativity and its long-term benefits. In effect, this approach is the antithesis of leading humanely. On the contrary, leaders should build a long-lasting legacy of accomplishment that is institutionalized for posterity. They owe their institutions and their followers a healthy existence and the relationships and reputation that enable a continuity of that healthy existence. Educational administrators are also responsible for future leadership. They need to identify, develop, and nurture future leaders to carry on the legacy.

Along with being responsible for providing future leaders, administrators owe the individuals in their institutions certain other legacies. Leaders need to be concerned with the institutional value system that determines the principles and standards that guide the practices of those in the organization. Administrators need to model their value systems so that individuals in the organization can learn to transmit these values to their colleagues and to future employees. In a civilized institution, we see good manners, respect for people, and an appreciation of the way in which we serve one another. Humane, sensitive, and thoughtful leaders will transmit their value systems through their daily behavior.

Administrators are obliged to provide and maintain direction by developing a vision. I made the point earlier that effective leaders must leave their organizations with a legacy. Part of this legacy should be a sense of progress or momentum. An educational administrator, for instance, should imbue his or her institution with a sense of continuous progress—a sense of constant improvement. Improvement and momentum come from a clear vision of what the institution ought to be, from a well-planned strategy to achieve that vision, and from carefully developed and articulated directions and plans that allow everyone to participate and be personally accountable for achieving those plans. Here is where functionalism and critical humanism intertwine. An institution cannot be humane if it is in chaos. It needs to operate effectively and efficiently.

Leaders are also responsible for effectiveness by being enablers. They need to enable others to reach their potential both personally and institutionally. I believe that the most effective ways of enabling one's colleagues is through participative decision making. It begins with believing in the potential of people, in their diversity of gifts. Leaders must realize that to maximize their own power and effectiveness, they need to empower others. Leaders are responsible for setting and attaining the goals in their organizations. Empowering or enabling others to help achieve those goals enhances the leader's chances of attaining the goals, ultimately enhancing the leader's effectiveness. Paradoxically, giving up power really amounts to gaining power.

THE CRITICAL TRADITION

A postpositivist leader combines the humanist tradition with critical theory. Dissatisfaction with current administrative approaches for examining social life stems from administrations' inability to deal with questions of value and morality and to fulfill their promise. For example, Griffiths criticizes orthodox theories because they "ignore the presence of unions and fail to account for the scarcity of women and minorities in top administrative positions."[2] Erickson asks, "Why has educational research had so few real implications for educational policy?" and answer that an empiricist research program modeled on the natural sciences fails to address issues of understanding and interpretation.[3] This failure precludes researchers from reaching a genuine understanding of the human condition. It is time, they argue, to treat educational research as a moral science. The science of administration can also be a moral one, a critically moral one.

The term moral is being used here in its cultural, professional, spiritual, and ethical sense, not in a religious sense. The moral side of administration has to do with the dilemmas that face us in education. All educators face three areas of dilemmas: control, curricular, and societal. Control dilemmas involve the resolution of classroom-management and control issues, particularly the issue of who is in charge and to what degree. Control dilemmas center around four questions:

1. Do you treat the child as a student, focusing narrowly on cognitive goals, or as a whole person, focusing more broadly on intellectual, aesthetic, social, and physical dimensions?
2. Who controls classroom time? In some classrooms, children are given latitude in scheduling their activities; in others, class activities follow a strict and mandatory schedule.
3. Who controls operations, or what larger context of what it means to be human and how we resolve the inevitable goes on in the classroom?
4. Who controls the standards and defines success and failure?

Similar dilemmas occur in the curricular domain and relate to whether the curriculum is considered as received, public knowledge or as private, individualized knowledge of the type achieved through discoveries and experiments. These curricular difficulties also depend on whether one conceives of the child as customer or as an individual. The customer receives professional services generated from a body of knowledge, whereas the individual receives personal services generated from his or her particular needs and context.

A final set of dilemmas has to do with what children bring to school and how they are to be treated once there. One concerns the distribution of teacher resources. Should one focus more resources on the less talented in order to bring them up to standards, or on the more talented in order for them to reach their full potential? The same question arises in regard to the distribution of justice. Should classroom rules be applied uniformly without regard to the differing circumstances of each child, or should family background, economic factors, and other sociological influences be considered? Should a teacher stress a common culture or ethnic differences and subculture consciousness?

Much of teaching involves resolving such dilemmas by making a variety of decisions throughout the school day. Such decisions can be made, however, in a reflective or an unreflective manner. An unreflective manner means simply teaching as one was taught, without giving consideration to available alternatives. A reflective approach involves an examination of the widest array of alternatives. Thus, reflective teaching suggests that dilemmas need not simply be resolved, but can be transformed, so that a higher level of teaching expertise is reached.

This same logic can be applied to administration. Administration involves the resolution of various dilemmas, that is, the making of moral decisions. One set of dilemmas involves control. How much participation can teachers have in the administration of the school? How much participation can parents and students have? Who evaluates and for what purpose? Is the role of administration collegial or authority-centered? The area of the curriculum brings up similar questions. Is the school oriented to basic skills, advanced skills, social skills, or all three? Should the curricula be teacher-made or nationally, state-, or system-mandated? Should student evaluation be based on teacher assessment or standardized tests? What is authentic assessment? Finally, an additional set of dilemmas pertains to the idea of schooling in society. Should the schools be oriented to ameliorate the apparent deficits that some students bring with them, or should they see different cultures and groups as strengths? Should schools be seen as agents of change, oriented to the creation of a more just society, or as socializers that adapt the young to the current social structure?

Oftentimes, these questions are answered unreflectively and simply resolved on an as-needed basis. This approach often resolves the dilemma, but does not foster a real transformation in one's self, role, or institution. If administration and leadership encompasses transformation, and I would argue that it should, then an additional lens to structural functionalism must be found through which these questions can be viewed. We suggest that the additional lens take the form of critical humanism and the Ignatian vision. In this context, then, administrative leadership can be viewed as a moral science.

NOTES

1. Max De Pree, *Leadership Is an Art* (New York: Dell Publishing, 1989).

2. D. Griffiths and Peter Ribbins, Leadership Matters in Education: Regarding Secondary Headship. (1995) Inaugural lecture, University of Birmingham, Edgbaston.

3. F. Erickson, "School Literacy, Reasoning and Civility: An Anthropologist's Perspective," *Review of Educational Research* 54 (1984): 525–546.

CHAPTER 5

The Ignatian Vision

More than 450 years ago, Ignatius of Loyola, a young priest born to an aristocratic Spanish family, founded the Society of Jesus, the Jesuits, and wrote his seminal book, *The Spiritual Exercises.*[1] In this book, he suggested a way of life and of looking at things that has been propagated by his religious community and other followers for almost five centuries. His principles have been utilized in a variety of ways. They have been used as an aid in developing one's own spiritual life; they have been used to formulate a way of learning that has become the curriculum and instructional method employed in the sixty Jesuit high schools and the twenty-eight Jesuit colleges and universities in the United States; and, they have been used to develop one's own administrative style. Together, these principles comprise the Ignatian vision.

There are five Ignatian principles that I wish to explore here as a foundation for developing an administrative philosophy and leadership style: (1) Ignatius's concept of the *magis*, or the "more"; (2) the implications of his notion of *cura personalis*, or "care of the person"; (3) the process of inquiry or discernment; (4) the development of men and women for others; and (5) service to the underserved and marginalized, or his concept of social justice.

At the core of the Ignatian vision is the concept of the *magis*, or the "more." Ignatius spent the greater part of his life seeking perfection in all areas of his personal, spiritual, and professional life. He was never satisfied with the status quo. He was constantly seeking to improve his own spiritual life, as well as his secular life as the leader of a growing religious community. He was an advocate of "continuous improvement" long before it became a corporate slogan, long before people like Edwards Deming used it to develop his total quality management approach to management, and long before Japan used it to revolutionize its economy after World War II.

The idea of constantly seeking "the more" implies change. The *magis* is a movement away from the status quo; and moving away from the status quo defines change. The Ignatian vision requires individuals and institutions to embrace the process of change as a vehicle for personal and institutional improvement. For his followers, frontiers and boundaries are not obstacles or ends, but new challenges to be faced, new opportunities to be welcomed. Thus, change needs to become a way of life. Ignatius further implores his followers to "be the change that you expect in others." In other words, we are called to model desired behavior—to live out our values, to be of ever fuller service to our communities, and to aspire to the more universal good. Ignatius had no patience with mediocrity. He constantly strove for the greater good.

The *magis* principle, then, can be described as the main norm in the selection of information and the interpretation of it. Every real alternative for choice must be conducive to the advancement toward perfection. When some aspect of a particular alternative is more conducive to reaching perfection than other alternatives, we have reason to choose that alternative. In the last chapter, we spoke of the dilemmas that educators face during every working day. The *magis* principle is a way of seeing that can help us select the better alternative.

At first hearing, the *magis* principle may sound rigid and frightening. It is absolute, and Ignatius is unyielding in applying it, but not rigid. On the one hand, he sees it as the expression of our love of humanity, which inexorably seeks to fill all of us with a desire to not be content with what is less good for us. On the other hand, he sees that humanity not only has its particular gifts, but also its limitations and different stages of growth. A choice that in the abstract would be more humane than it would be in the concrete would not be seen as adhering to the *magis* principle. For example, tracking students according to ability can be seen as humane in the abstract, but in the concrete can be dehumanizing. Ignatius would advise us to focus on the concrete in resolving this dilemma.

In every case, then, accepting and living by the *magis* principle is an expression of our love of humanity. So, whatever the object for choice, the measure of our love of our neighbor will be the fundamental satisfaction we will find in choosing and acting by the *magis* principle. Whatever one chooses by this principle, no matter how undesirable in some other respect, will always be what one would most want as a moral and ethical member of the human race.

Closely related to the principle of the *magis* is the Ignatian principle of inquiry and discernment. In his writings, he urges us to challenge the status quo through the methods of inquiry and discernment. This is very similar to one of the tenants of critical theory. In fact the Ignatian vision and critical theory share a number of norms.

To Ignatius, the need to enter into inquiry and discernment is to determine God's will. However, this process is of value for the purely secular purpose of deciding on which "horn of a dilemma" one should come down. To aid us in utilizing inquiry and discernment as useful tools in challenging the status quo and determining the right choice to be made, Ignatius suggests that the ideal disposition for inquiry and discernment is humility. The disposition of humility is especially helpful when, despite one's best efforts, the evidence that one alternative is more conducive to the betterment of society is not compelling. When the discerner cannot find evidence to show that one alternative is more conducive to the common good, Ignatius calls for a judgment in favor of what more assimilates the discerner's life to the life of poverty and humiliation. Thus, when the greatest good cannot readily be determined, the greater good is more easily discerned in the position of humility. These are very demanding standards, but they are consistent with the *magis* principle and the tenets of critical humanism.

In addition to the *magis* principle norm, taking account of what has just been said and of what was said earlier about the norm of humility as a disposition for seeking the greater good, the relationship of the greater good norm to the greatest good norm can be clarified. The latter is absolute, overriding, always primary. The greater good norm is secondary; it can never, in any choice, have equal weight with the first *magis* principle; it can never justify a choice of actual poverty and humiliation over riches and honors if the latter are seen to be more for the service of humanity in a particular situation or choice, with all its concrete circumstances, including the agent's responsibilities to others and his or her own stage of psychological and spiritual development. In other words, if being financially successful allows one to serve the poor and underserved better, that would be preferred to actual poverty.

Ignatius presents us with several other supplemental norms for facing our dilemmas. In choices that directly affect the individual person and the underserved or marginalized, especially the poor, Ignatius urges us to give preference to those in need. This brings us to his next guiding principle, *cura personalis* or "care of the person."

Another of Ignatius's important and enduring principles is his notion that, despite the primacy of the common good, the need to care for the individual person should never be lost. From the very beginning, the *cura personalis* principle has been included in the mission statement of virtually every high school and college founded by the Jesuits. It also impacts the method of instruction suggested for all Jesuit schools in the *ratio studiorum*, or the "course of study," in these institutions. All Jesuit educational institutions are to foster what we now refer to as a constructivist classroom, where the student is an active participant in the learning process. This contrasts with the transmission method of instruction where the teacher is paramount, and the student is a passive participant in the process. In the Ignatian vision, the care of the person is a requirement not only on a personal-needs basis, but also on a whole-person basis, which would, of course, include classroom education.

This principle also has implications for how we conduct ourselves as educational administrators. Ignatius calls us to value the gifts and charisms of our colleagues and to address any deficiencies that they might have and turn them into strengths. For example, during the employee evaluation process, Ignatius would urge us to focus on the formative stage of the evaluation far more than on the summative stage. This would be one small way of applying *cura personalis* theory to practice.

The fourth principle that we wish to consider is the Ignatian concept of service. Once again, this principle has been propagated from the very outset. The expressed goal of virtually every Jesuit institution is "to develop men and women for others." Jesuit institutions are called on to create a culture of service as one way of ensuring that the students, faculty, and staff of these institutions reflect the educational, civic, and spiritual values of the Ignatian vision.

Institutions following the Ignatian tradition of service to others have done so through community services programs, and more recently, service learning. Service to the community provides students with a means of helping others, a way to put their value system into action, and a tangible way to assist local communities. Although these were valuable benefits, there was no formal integration of the service experience into the curriculum and no formal introspection concerning the impact of service on the individual. During the last ten years, there has been a movement toward creating a more intentional academic relationship. Service has evolved from a modest student activity into an exciting pedagogical opportunity. In the past, service was viewed as a cocurricular activity; today, it plays an integral role in the learning process.

Because many institutions are situated in an urban setting, service gives them a chance to share resources with surrounding communities and allows for reciprocal relationships to form between the university and local residents. Immersion into different cultures—economic, racial, educational, social, and religious—is the vehicle by which students make connections. Working side-by-side with people of varying backgrounds significantly impacts the students, forcing them outside of their comfort zones and into the gritty reality of how others live. Through reflection, these students have the opportunity to integrate these powerful experiences into their lives, opening their eyes and hearts to the larger questions of social justice. Peter-Hans Kolvenbach, the Superior General of the Jesuit order, in his address on justice in American Jesuit universities in October 2000, used the words of Pope John Paul II to challenge Jesuit educators to "educate the whole person of solidarity for the real world" not only through concepts learned in the classroom, but also by contact with real people.[2]

Upon assuming the position of Superior General in 1973 and echoing the words of Ignatius, Pedro Arrupe declared "our prime educational objective must be to form men and women for others; men and women who will live not for themselves but for others. . ." In the spirit of these words, the service-learning movement has legitimized the educational benefit of all experiential activity. The term service learning means different things to different people, and debates on service learning have been around for decades, running the gamut from unstructured programmatic opportunities to structured educational philosophies. At Ignatian institutions, service learning is a bridge that connects faculty, staff, and students with community partners and their agency needs. It connects academic and student life views about the educational value of experiential learning. It also connects students' textbooks to human reality, and their minds and hearts with values and action. The programs are built on key components of service learning, including integration into the curriculum, a reciprocal relationship between the community agency and student, and structured time for reflection, which is very much related to the Ignatian principle of discernment discussed earlier.

Participation in service by high school and college students, whether as a cocurricular or a course-based experience, correlates to where they are in their developmental process. Service work allows students to explore their skills and limitations, to find what excites and energizes them, to put their values into action, and to use their talents to benefit others, to discover who they are and whom they want to become. By encouraging students to reflect on their service, these institutions assist in this self-discovery. The reflection can take many forms: an informal chat, a facilitated group discussion, written dialogue, journal entries, reaction papers, or in-class presentations on articles. By integrating the service experience through critical reflection, the student develops self-knowledge of the communities in which he or she lives and knowledge about the world that surrounds them. It is only after the unfolding of this service-based knowledge that the students are able to synthesize what they have learned with their lives. Through this reflection, the faculty members also have an opportunity to learn from and about their students. Teachers witness the change and growth of the students first hand. In short, "service to others" changes lives.

The implications of "service to others" for administration are clear. Not only can educational administrators enhance their effectiveness by including the idea of service to others in their curricula, but also by modeling it in their personal and professional lives. The concept of administrators becoming the "servant of the servants" is what I have in mind here. Servant leaders do not inflict pain, they bear pain, and they treat their employees as volunteers, a concept that we will explore more fully later.

The Ignatian concept of service leads into his notion of solidarity with the underserved (poor) and marginalized and his principle of social justice. We begin our discussion with an attempt to clarify the nature and role of social justice in the Ignatian vision. According to some, Ignatius defined justice in both a narrow and a wide sense.[3] In the narrow sense, it involves "justice among men and women." In this case, it is a matter of "clear obligations" among "members of the human family." The application of this kind of justice includes not only the rendering of material goods, but also of immaterial goods, such as "reputation, dignity, the possibility of exercising freedom."[4]

Many of his followers also believe Ignatius defined justice in a wider sense "where situations are encountered which are humanly intolerable and demand a remedy."[5] Here the situations may be a product of "explicitly unjust acts" caused by "clearly identified people" who cannot be obliged to correct the injustices, yet the dignity of the human person requires that justice be restored; or they may be caused by nonidentifiable people. It is precisely within the structural forces of inequality in society where injustice of this second type is found, where injustice is institutionalized, that is, built into economic, social, and political structures both national and international, and where people are suffering from poverty and hunger, from the unjust distribution of wealth, resources, and power. The critical theorists of whom we spoke earlier would likely concur with this wider definition of social justice.

It is almost certain that Ignatius did not only concern himself with injustices that were purely economic. He often cites injustices about "threats to human life and its quality," "racial and political discrimination," and loss of respect for the "rights of individuals or groups."[6] When one adds to these the "vast range of injustices" enumerated in his writings, one sees that the Ignatian vision understands its mission of justice to include "the widest possible view of justice," involving every area where there is an attack on human rights. We can conclude, therefore, that although Ignatius was to some degree concerned about commutative justice (right relationships between private persons and groups) and distributive justice (the obligations of the state to render to the individual what is his or her due), he is most concerned about what is generally called today social justice, or "justice of the common good." Such justice is comprehensive and includes the above strict legal rights and duties, but is more concerned about the natural rights and duties of individuals, families, communities, and the community of nations toward one another as members of the common family of human beings. Every form of justice is included in and presupposed by social justice, but with social justice, it is the social nature of the person that is emphasized, as well as the social significance of all earthly goods, the purpose of which is to aid all members of the human community to attain their dignity as human beings. Many of Ignatius's followers believe that this dignity is being undermined in our world today, and their main efforts are aimed toward restoring that dignity.

In the pursuit of social justice, Ignatius calls on his followers to be "in solidarity with the poor." The next logical question might then be, who are the poor? The poor are usually thought to be those who are economically deprived and politically oppressed. Thus, we can conclude that the promotion of justice means working to overcome the oppressions or injustices that make the poor poor. The fallacy here, however, is that the poor are not necessarily oppressed or suffering injustice, and so Ignatius argues that our obligation toward the poor must be understood as referring to those suffering "inhuman levels of poverty and injustice" and not as concerned with the "lot of those possessing only modest resources," even though those of modest means are often poor and oppressed. So, we conclude that the poor include those who are "wrongfully" impoverished or dispossessed.[7]

An extended definition of the poor, one that Ignatius would espouse, would include any of these types of people:

1. Those who are economically deprived and socially marginalized and oppressed, especially, but not limited to, those with whom one has immediate contact and is in a position to affect positively
2. Those who are "poor in spirit"; that is, those who lack a value system or an ethical and moral sense
3. Those who are emotionally poor, who have psychological and emotional shortcomings and are in need of comfort

In defining the poor in the broadest way, Ignatius exhorts us to undertake social change in our role as leaders, to do what we can do to bring an end to inequality, oppression, and injustice. Once again, we can see the close connection between the Ignatian principles of social justice and the main tenets of critical theory.

IMPLICATIONS FOR ADMINISTRATION

Each of the principles of the Ignatian vision noted above has a variety of implications for educational administrators. The *magis* principle has implications for administrators in that it calls for us to be seeking perfection continually in all that we do. In effect, this means that we must seek to improve continually. And, because improvement implies change, we need to be champions of needed change in our institutions. This means that we have to model a tolerance for change and embrace not only our own change initiatives, but also those in other parts of the organization. An in depth application of the Ignatian vision to the process of change will be discussed later.

The principle of *cura personalis* has additional implications. To practice the Ignatian vision, one must treat people with dignity under all circumstances. *Cura personalis* also requires us to extend ourselves in offering individual attention and attending to the needs of all those with whom we come into contact. Being sensitive to the individual's unique needs is particularly required. Many times, in our efforts to treat people equally, we actually fail to treat them fairly and equitably. Certain individuals have greater needs than others, and many times these needs require that exceptions be made on their behalf. For example, if an adult student does not hand in an assignment on time, but the tardiness is due to the fact that he or she is going through some personal trauma at the moment, the principle of *cura personalis* calls on us to make an exception in this case. It is likely that many would consider such an exception to be unfair to those who made the effort to complete the assignment in a timely manner or that we cannot possibly be sensitive to the special needs of all of our students and colleagues. However, as long as the exception is made for anyone in the same circumstances, Ignatius would not perceive this exception as being unfair. In fact, the exception would be expected if one is practicing the principle of care of the person.

The Ignatian process of discernment requires educational administrators to be reflective practitioners. It calls on us to be introspective regarding our administrative and leadership behavior. We are asked to reflect on the ramifications of our decisions, especially in light of their cumulative effect on the equitable distribution of power and on the marginalized individuals and groups in our communities. In effect, the principle of discernment galvanizes the other principles embodied in the Ignatian vision. During the discernment process, we are asked to reflect upon how our planned behavior will manifest the *magis* principle, *cura personalis*, and service to the community, to especially the underserved, marginalized, and oppressed.

The development of men and women for others requires the leader to have his or her own sense of service toward those with whom he or she interacts and that the leader also develop this spirit of service in others. The concept of servant leadership requires us to encourage others toward a life and career of service and to assume the position of being the servant of the servants. Ignatius thinks about leadership in terms of what the gospel writer Luke calls the "one who serves." The leader owes something to the institution he or she leads. The leader is seen in this context as steward rather than owner or proprietor.

The implications of Ignatius's notion of social justice are myriad for the administrator. Being concerned about the marginalized among our constituencies is required. We are called upon to be sensitive to those individuals and groups that do not share equitably in the distribution of power and influence. Participative decision making and collaborative behavior is encouraged among administrators imbued with the Ignatian tradition. Equitable representation of all segments of the school community should be provided whenever feasible. Leadership behavior such as this will assure that the dominant culture is not perpetuated to the detriment of the minority culture, rendering the minorities powerless. We will discuss additional ways of applying these principles to one's practice in later chapters.

NOTES

1. Andre Ravier, SJ, *Ignatius of Loyola and the Founding of the Society of Jesus* (San Francisco: Ignatius Press, 1987).

2. Martin R. Tripole, SJ, *Faith Beyond Justice* (St. Louis: The Institute of Jesuit Sources, 1994).

3. Jules J. Toner, SJ, *Discerning God's Will: Ignatius of Loyola's Teaching on Christian Decision Making* (St. Louis: The Institute of Jesuit Sources, 1991).

4. Martin R. Tripole, SJ, *Faith Beyond Justice* (St. Louis: The Institute of Jesuit Sources, 1994).

5. Martin R. Tripole, SJ, *Faith Beyond Justice* (St. Louis: The Institute of Jesuit Sources, 1994).

6. Christopher Chapple, *The Jesuit Tradition in Education and Missions* (Scranton: University of Scranton Press, 1993).

7. *Documents of the 34th General Congregation of the Society of Jesus* (St. Louis: The Institute of Jesuit Sources, 1995).

CHAPTER 6

Implications for Organizational Development

Educational practitioners are often critical of theoretical concepts, such as critical theory and the Ignatian vision, because although their principles are acceptable, and even laudable, their proponents never seem to suggest meaningful ways of applying these principles. In this chapter we suggest ways of effectively applying these theories to the development of an organization, such as an educational institution. We are suggesting here that the organizational health of an educational institution is determined by how effectively the following aspects of the organization are developed and implemented:

1. Structure
2. Culture
3. Leadership
4. Motivation
5. Communication
6. Conflict management
7. Decision making
8. Distribution of power
9. Strategic planning
10. Change

We will suggest addressing these components of the institution using structural-functionalist strategies, but examining them through the lens of critical theory and the Ignatian vision.

ORGANIZATIONAL STRUCTURE

Educational institutions are essentially organized according to one of three basic structures: the classical structure, the social-systems structure, or the open-system structure. Despite being primarily organized around one of these structures, most schools and school systems reflect certain aspects of each of these models.[1]

Classical theorists believe that the application of a bureaucratic structure and process will promote rational, efficient, and disciplined behavior, making possible the achievement of well-defined goals. Efficiency, then, is achieved by arranging positions and jurisdiction and by placing power at the top of a clear chain of command. The conceptual model of the classical theory has had a significant impact on education. Virtually every educational institution in the United States is organized according to the tenets of the classical theory. For example, classical theory calls for a hierarchy with graded levels of authority. Schools have responded to this aspect of classical theory by setting up levels of control beginning with the school board and flowing down to the superintendent, the principals, the teachers, and the students.

Within the classical-theory framework, the individual is regarded as an object, a part of the bureaucratic machine. This is the antithesis of critical theory and the Ignatian vision. A more acceptable organizational structure would be one based on social-systems theory. Historically, researchers found that the impact of social-psychological variables within the worker group was significant. The study of behavior in social-system settings intensified, and greater sophistication developed about how and why group members behave as they do under given conditions. In time, a natural social-systems orientation to the analysis of behavior evolved in the literature as an alternative to the rational or classical systems approach.

The conceptual perspective of the social-systems model suggests that an organization consists of a collection of groups (social systems) that collaborate to achieve system goals. Coalitions among subgroups within the organization, such as the primary-grade teachers, form to provide power bases upon which positive or negative action can be taken; for example, "Let's lobby the principal to introduce technology in the primary grades." As with the classical organizational theory, schools and school systems have been profoundly influenced by the social-systems model.

A newer theory that is having a growing influence on educational institutions, especially higher education, is the open-system model. The classical and social-systems theories tend to view organizational life as a closed system, isolated from the surrounding environment. In contrast, open-system theory regards an organization as a set of interrelated parts that interact with the environment. It receives "input" (human and material resources, values, community expectations, and societal demands), transforms them through a "production process" (an educational program), and exports the product in the form of "output" (graduates, new knowledge, revised value sets) into the environment (businesses, the military, homes) with "value added." The organization receives a return (community financial support in the form of taxes or tuition) for its efforts so it can survive and prosper. Then, the cycle begins once again with the new students entering the school.

Through the perspective of open-system theory, a new logic of issues of organizational governance has emerged. It emphasizes the relationship of the organization to its surrounding environment and, thus, places a premium on planning and programming for events that cannot be controlled directly. The key to making an open system work effectively and efficiently is its ability to gather, process, and utilize information. In an educational institution, then, the facility with which a need is discovered, a goal is established, and resources are coalesced to meet that need will determine the effectiveness and efficiency of that institution. Unlike businesses, educational institutions, especially colleges and universities, have not yet found a way to meet the demands of the open-system model.

Knowing how one's individual educational entity is structured within the context of these three models is the first step in an educational leader's quest to truly "know the territory" of his or her institution. The very latest research indicates that none of these models, in and of itself, is an effective organizational structure. On the contrary, a combination of these models has been shown to be most effective. There is a need in most institutions for roles to be defined (classical theory), but there is also a need for relationships to be considered (social-systems theory) and for groups to collaborate (open-system theory). It is the responsibility of the leader to develop the organizational structure that is appropriate and effective in his or her situation. By doing so, the leader will have taken the first step in the process of insuring the organizational good health of the institution.

Diagnostic Checklist

Here are some questions that can be addressed in assessing your institution's organizational structure through the lens of structural functionalism, critical theory, and the Ignatian vision:

- Is there appropriate division of labor and is it flexible?
- Is the division of labor conducive to reaching organizational goals?
- Is the structure of the organization well designed?
- Do work groups operate and communicate effectively?
- Are the best aspects of the classical, social-systems, and open-system organizational models present?
- Does the organization's structure respond to external and internal environmental contingencies?
- Does the structure of the organization marginalize various individuals or groups?
- Does the structure of the organization treat people humanely?
- Does the structure ensure the equitable distribution of power and influence?
- Is the structure flexible enough to adapt to continuous progress and change?

ORGANIZATIONAL CULTURE

The next consideration in ensuring the organizational good health of an institution is its organizational culture. Organizational culture can be defined as the shared beliefs, expectations, values, and norms of conduct of its members. In any organization, the informal culture interacts with the formal structure and control system to produce a generally clear understanding of the "way things are done around here." Even more than the forces of bureaucracy, the organization's culture is the glue that binds people and groups together.

Anyone who has visited a number of educational institutions develops a sense of their different "personalities," or cultures. In walking the hallways and campus of an educational institution, an astute observer can see physical manifestations of an underlying set of values: perhaps a huge trophy case in the entrance lobby; classroom desks bolted to the floor; a clean and attractive campus; football, basketball, and band programs that overshadow academic programs; faculty and staff constantly patrolling the halls; clandestine meetings of students or faculty.

The above are tangible aspects of the school's culture. The intangible aspects often parallel those values. Schools attempting to develop shared values and enculturate them often illustrate them by symbols frequently found around the campus: "Knowledge Is Power," "Wildcat Pride," "Education Is About Alternative," "Just Say No," and "All Children Achieving." Other symbols of the school's culture are the heroes and storytellers that we will speak more of in the next chapter. Other important components of a school's culture include the dominant attribution process in the institution: Do individuals tend to have an internal or external locus of control? Do they tend to blame outside forces for their deficiencies? Do they internalize the blame and try to improve?

The attitude of the faculty and staff, along with how they perceive their environment, are other important components of the institution's culture. Do they have a positive or negative predisposition? Do perceptual distortions, like stereotyping, projection, and the halo effect proliferate?

Another important component of organizational culture is the learning processes in an institution. Just as students have different learning styles, so do adults. So, the question is, how can school administrators encourage their own and others' learning in the workplace and transform the school into what Peter Senge calls the "learning organization?"[2] They can ensure that appropriate conditions for learning exist; providing appropriate stimuli (e.g., professional development materials) should facilitate acquisition of the skills or attitudes desired. Administrators should reinforce desired learned behaviors. They should also provide environmental cues that encourage learning. Structuring a context that supports learning is essential. In effect, just as we advise teachers to adapt their teaching styles to the learning styles of their students, administrators must adapt their management styles to the variety of learning styles that are present in their institutions.

Administrators can use the following modeling strategy. First, the administrator should identify the goal or target behaviors that will lead to improved performance. For example, a more extensive use of cooperative learning strategies will lead to improving students' social skills. Second, the administrator must select the appropriate model and determine whether to present the model through a live demonstration, videotape, other media, or a combination of all of these. Third, the administrator must make sure the teachers are capable of meeting the technical skill requirements of the target behavior. For example, further training might be necessary. Fourth, the administrator must structure a favorable and positive learning environment to increase the likelihood that the teachers will learn the new behavior and act in the desired way. Starting cooperative learning with a particularly skilled teacher and a cooperative group of students increases the chances of success. Fifth, the administrator must model the target behavior and carry out supporting activities, such as role playing. Conducting a faculty meeting using cooperative-learning techniques would be an example of such a strategy. Sixth, the administrator should positively reinforce reproduction of the target behaviors both in training and in the workplace. Teacher-of-the-month awards are an example of this strategy. Once the target behaviors are reproduced, administrators must maintain and strengthen them through a system of rewards until the behavior is institutionalized, that is, until it becomes part of the school culture.

Although all of the above considerations are important in assessing and improving an institution's culture, perhaps the most important component of organizational culture is the presence of, or the lack of, trust and respect among the organization's members, especially between the administration and the faculty and staff. Achieving educational effectiveness is an incremental, sequential improvement process. This improvement process begins by building security within each individual so that he or she can be flexible in adapting to changes within education. Addressing only skills or techniques, such as communication, motivation, negotiation, or empowerment, is ineffective when individuals in an organization do not trust its systems, themselves, or one another. An institution's resources are wasted when invested only in training programs that assist administrators in mastering quick-fix techniques that, at best, attempt to manipulate employees and, at worst, reinforce mistrust.

The challenge is to transform relationships based on insecurity, adversarialism, and politics to those based on mutual trust. Trust is the beginning of effectiveness and forms the foundation of a principle-centered learning environment that places emphasis upon strengths and devises innovative methods to minimize weaknesses. The transformation process requires an internal locus of control that emphasizes individual responsibility and accountability for change and for promoting effectiveness.

Diagnostic Checklist

Here are some questions that can be addressed in assessing your institution's organizational culture through the lens of structural functionalism, critical theory, and the Ignatian vision:

- Does the organization exhibit a culture of mutual trust and respect?
- Do perceptual distortions proliferate?
- Does the workforce exhibit an internal locus of control?
- Is the institution a learning organization?
- Are the various learning styles being addressed in the management process?
- What beliefs and values do the individuals in the organization have?
- Do the beliefs and attitudes conform to the principles of critical theory and the Ignatian vision?
- How do these beliefs and values influence individual attitudes?
- What functional and dysfunctional behaviors result from the individuals' attitudes?
- Is there a climate of participative decision making?
- Is there a caring atmosphere present?
- Is there a respect for diversity in all of its expressions?
- Are the faculty and staff interested in continuous progress (magis)?

ORGANIZATIONAL LEADERSHIP

In chapter 1, I addressed the question of leadership and proposed a definition with which I would work in the context of this text. Recently, a plethora of research studies have been conducted on leadership and leadership styles. The overwhelming evidence indicates that there is no one singular leadership style that is most appropriate in all situations. Rather, an administrator's leadership style should be adapted to the situation so that at various times task behavior or relationship behavior might be appropriate. At other times and in other situations, various degrees of both task and relationship behavior may be most effective.

The emergence of transformational leadership has seen leadership theory come full circle. Transformational-leadership theory combines aspects of the early trait theory perspective with the more current situational or contingency models. The personal charisma of the leader, along with his or her ability to formulate an educational vision and to communicate it to others, determines the transformational leader's effectiveness.

Because the effective leader is expected to adapt his or her leadership style to an ever-changing environment, administration becomes an even more complex and challenging task. However, a thorough knowledge of leadership theory can make some sense of the apparent chaos that the administrator faces on an almost daily basis.

From a structural-functionalist viewpoint, transformational leaders would simply need to practice the research-based skills that have been found to be effective. Thus, they would develop a mission and a vision, establish goals and objectives, and implement them by employing leadership behaviors that are appropriate to the situation. However, the critical pedagogues and followers of Ignatian pedagogy would posit that if a leader confines his or her thinking to the technical aspects of leadership, the leader will not maximize his or her impact. They would suggest that in addition to involving the mind in determining their behavior, leaders should also involve the heart and soul in the process. Thus, such concerns as "care of the person," equitable distribution of power and influence, social justice, and identification with the oppressed and marginalized should be considered in determining one's leadership behavior.

Diagnostic Checklist

Here are some questions that can be addressed in assessing your institution's structure and culture through the lens of structural functionalism, critical theory, and the Ignatian vision:

- Do the administrators display the behaviors required for effective leadership?

- Do the leaders encourage the appropriate amount of participation in decision making?
- Does the leadership adapt to the task and the maturity level of the followers?
- Do transformational leaders exist?
- Do they operate in the various frames of leadership?
- Do they articulate a vision and a strategic plan?
- Are they sensitive to the needs of individuals?
- Are they inclusive in their dealings with the faculty and staff?
- Do they view the institution as a vehicle for social change?

MOTIVATING FACULTY AND STAFF

The next step in preparing oneself to be an effective administrator is to adopt an approach to motivate one's colleagues to attain the educational vision that has been jointly developed. To begin the process, you might ask yourself what motivates individuals to behave, think, or feel in certain ways. What factors make you or others more willing to work, to be creative, to achieve, to produce? Theory and research in the area of motivation provide a systematic way of diagnosing the degree of motivation and of prescribing ways of increasing it. There are basically two views of motivation. One view posits that individuals are motivated by inherited, conflicting, and unconscious drives. This view, which was popularized by Freud and Jung, and more recently by Skinner, Maslow, and Glasser, is operationalized through the so called content theories of motivation, such as the various needs theories.

The other view of motivation says that an individual is basically rational and is normally conscious of his or her pursuit of goals. Plato and Aristotle, and more recently Jerome Bruner, are associated with this view. This perspective has spawned the so-called process theories of motivation, including the equity theory, expectancy theory, and goal-setting theory.

Suppose the president of a college makes $150,000 per year and a faculty member earns $75,000. And suppose this college decided to base part of its annual salary increases on whether it met its recruitment quota. Why would such a college think this policy might motivate its employees? Early motivation theorists would explain such a situation by saying that the college expects the new policy to meet the employee's needs—their basic requirement for living and working productively. As the work force in organizations becomes more diverse, recognizing the individuality of needs becomes paramount; identifying and responding to them becomes a critical issue in effective management.

How do we identify employees' needs? To do a good job of identifying them, we probably would need to spend a great deal of time talking with the employees and observing their behavior both in and out of the work environment. Many times, determining employees' needs outside of the work environment is conjecture. But the effort should be made so that the leader has a better chance of identifying, and then meeting, the needs of his or her colleagues.

In 1935, Abraham Maslow developed the first needs theory, which is still one of the most popular and well-known motivation theories. Maslow stated that individuals have five needs, arranged in a hierarchy from the most basic to the highest level: physiological, safety, belongingness and love, esteem, and self-actualization.[3]

Physiological needs are the most basic needs an individual has. These include, at a minimum, a person's requirement for food, water, shelter, sex, the ability to care for his or her children, and medical and dental coverage. Safety needs include a person's desire for security or protection. This translates most directly into concerns for short-term and long-term job security, as well as physical safety at work. Belongingness and love needs focus on the social aspects of work and non-work situations. Virtually all individuals desire affectionate relationships or regular interaction with others, which can become a key facet of job design. Esteem needs relate to a person's desire to master his or her own work, demonstrate competence and accomplishments, build a reputation as an outstanding performer, hold a position of prestige, receive public recognition, and feel self-esteem. Self-actualization needs reflect an individual's desire to grow and develop to his or her fullest potential. An individual often wants the opportunity to be creative on the job or desires autonomy, responsibility, and challenge.

According to needs theory, organizations must meet unsatisfied needs in order for employees to be motivated. In Maslow's scheme, the lowest unsatisfied need, starting with the basic physiological needs and continuing through safety, belonging and love, esteem, and self-actualization needs, becomes the prepotent, or most powerful and significant, need.

Although the order may vary in certain special circumstances, generally the prepotent need motivates an individual to act to fulfill it; satisfied needs do not motivate. If, for example, a person lacks sufficient food and clothing, he or she will act to satisfy those basic physiological needs; hence, this person would most likely work to receive pay or other benefits to satisfy those needs. On the other hand, a person whose physiological, safety, and belongingness needs are satisfied will be motivated to satisfy needs at the next level, the esteem needs. For this person, pay will not motivate performance unless it increases esteem, but a promotion or other changes in a job's title or status, which satisfy esteem needs, are likely to motivate.

Administrators should understand that the popularity of this theory of motivation stems primarily from its simplicity and logic, not from strong current research support. In general, research indicates that two or three categories of needs, rather than five, exist, and that the relationships, relative importance, and sequences are not consistent from one individual to another. In addition, the ordering of needs may vary in different cultures. Thus, Maslow's theory may not be generalized across cultures.

Consider again the example of the college that attached some salary increases to whether it reached its recruitment goals. To use Maslow's theory to diagnose the likely effectiveness of the new policy, we can ask three questions: (1)Which needs have already been satisfied? (2) Which unsatisfied need is lowest in the hierarchy? (3) Can this need be satisfied with the new policy? If, for example, the physiological and safety needs have been satisfied, then the social needs become prepotent; if the new policy can satisfy those needs, which is unlikely, then, according to Maslow's theory, it would be motivating.

There are a number of needs-based theories, including Alderfer's Existence/Relatedness/Growth theory, McClelland's Trichotomy of Needs theory, Herzberg's two-factor theory, and Glasser's control theory. However, they are all rooted in Maslow's theory, and only differ from his theory in idiosyncratic ways.[4]

The second major type of motivation theory evolved from social-comparison theory. Lacking objective measures of performance or appropriate attitudes, individuals assess and compare their performance and attitudes with that of others. Equity theory assumes that people assess their job performance and attitudes by comparing both their contribution to work and the benefits they derive from work to the contributions and benefits of a comparison other, an individual whom the person selects and who in reality may be like or unlike the person. A high-school teacher, for example, might reasonably compare his or her effort and rewards to those of another teacher, but may in fact compare his or her effort to that of the principal, or even the superintendent.

Equity theory further states that a person is motivated in proportion to the perceived fairness of the rewards received for a certain amount of effort. You may have heard a student complain, "I'm going to stop studying so hard. Scott is brighter than I am, and he never seems to study and still gets A's." This student has compared his effort with Scott's and perceived an inequity in this school situation. In fact, no actual inequity may exist, but the perception of inequity influences the student's subsequent actions.

Specifically, this student compared his perceptions of two ratios: (1) the ratio of his outcomes to his inputs to (2) the ratio of another's outcomes to inputs. Outcomes may include pay, status, and job complexity; inputs include effort, productivity, age, sex, or experience. Thus, he or she may compare his pay-to-experience ratio to another's ratio, or their status-to-age ratio to another's. For example, employee A may feel that he or she receives $25 for each hour of effort. In contrast, he may assess that employee B receives $50 for each hour of effort. Employee A perceives that his ratio of outcomes to inputs (25 to 1) is less than employee B's (50 to 1). In fact, employee B may only receive $15 for each hour of effort he contributes to the job. But, according to equity theory, the facts do not influence motivation; perceptions of the situation do. Recent research suggests, however, that equity calculations may be difficult because of cognitive differences in assessment and performance. Instead, individuals look for long-term rather than short-term parity in work situations; they compare their rank order on merit and a scale of reward outcomes, and see equity as a goal to work for over time.

According to equity theory, individuals are motivated to reduce any perceived inequity. They strive to make these ratios equal by changing either the outcomes or the inputs. The student referred to above, for example, might reduce his inputs (his effort) to make the ratio the same as Scott's. If he cannot change his own inputs or outcomes, he might adjust either his perception of Scott's outcomes or inputs or his attitude toward the situation by reevaluating his effort or obtaining more accurate information about Scott's grades and study habits and adjusting the ratio accordingly.

In theory, the same adjustment process occurs when a person perceives that he or she receives too much reward for the input or has too complex a job in comparison to others. Thus, if a person believes that he or she is overpaid, the individual should either increase his or her effort or ask that his or her pay be decreased. Although early studies suggested that this would happen, recent research has questioned whether this over-justification effect really occurs.

While equity theory basically makes strong intuitive sense, the empirical evidence has been mixed. The concept of equity sensitivity in part explains these findings by suggesting that individuals have different preferences for equity (e.g., a preference for higher, lower, or equal ratios) that cause them to react consistently, but differently to perceived equity and inequity.

In a sense, equity theory over simplifies the motivational issues by not explicitly considering individual needs, values, or personalities. This oversimplification becomes particularly important as the work force becomes more diverse. Cross-cultural differences may occur in preferences for equity, as well as the preferred responses to inequitable situations.

To determine whether equity exists in the workplace, we can use a questionnaire, such as the Organizational Fairness Questionnaire.[5] If nothing else, equity theory makes a strong case for fairness in the workplace, which would please the critical theorists and those espousing the Ignatian vision.

Another process theory worth considering is expectancy theory. It has dominated research on motivation for some time because it has strong empirical support, integrates diverse perspectives on motivation, and provides explicit ways to increase employee motivation. Perhaps more than the preceding theories, expectancy theory offers a comprehensive view of motivation that integrates many of the elements of the needs, equity, and reinforcement theories. The research done in education regarding teacher expectations and students of all ages fulfilling these expectations is a compelling example of expectancy theory in practice.[6]

Victor Vroom popularized the expectancy theory in the 1960s with his model, which stated that motivation is a function of expectancy, valence, and instrumentality:

Motivation = Expectancy × Valence × Instrumentality

This simple formulation identifies the three basic components of expectancy theory. Expectancy refers to a person's perception of the probability that effort will lead to performance. For example, a person who perceives that if he or she works harder, then he or she will produce more has a high expectancy. An individual that perceives that if he or she works harder, he or she will be ostracized by other employees and will not receive the cooperation necessary for performing has a lower expectancy. If expectancy is zero, then motivation will be lower than if expectancy is positive.

Instrumentality refers to a person's perception of the probability that certain outcomes, positive or negative, will be attached to that performance. For example, a person who perceives that he or she will receive greater pay or benefits if he or she produces has a high instrumentality. Motivation is a function of the degree of instrumentality, in addition to expectancy and valence.

Valence refers to a person's perception of the value of specific outcomes, that is, how much the person likes or dislikes receiving these outcomes. An individual with high esteem needs will generally attach a high valence to a new job title or a promotion. When valence is high, motivation is likely to be higher than when valence is lower or negative.

Let us examine the case of a college professor using this formulation of motivation. If the college professor perceives that devoting more time to scholarly research will result in his or her performing better, expectancy will be positive. If the professor perceives that he or she will receive a promotion and a pay raise if he or she performs the job well, then the instrumentality is positive. If the professor likes receiving a promotion and a raise, then the valence will be positive. We can operationalize this equation by arbitrarily assigning values to each variable.

Because performance can lead to multiple outcomes, each with different valences or values, each performance-to-outcome expectancy is multiplied by the corresponding valence. For example, consider a new teacher who knows that if he or she demonstrates that considerable effort is being exerted to be productive in the classroom, he or she will have a contract renewal, resulting in a positive performance-to-outcome expectancy. But the teacher also knows that if he or she puts in too much time and effort, the teacher will be ostracized by coworkers for being a "pawn of the administration"; this performance-to-outcome expectancy is much less positive, and probably approaches zero. These products are summed before being multiplied by the effort-to-performance expectancy. If the sum of the formula is positive, the work environment is motivating; if it is a negative sum, the work environment is not motivating.

Although evidence for the validity of the expectancy model is mixed, managers can still use it to diagnose motivational problems or to evaluate effective motivation. Answers to the following questions should help administrators determine the level of an employee's work motivation, identify any deficiencies in the job situation, and prescribe remedies: (1) Does the individual perceive that effort will lead to performance? (2) Does the individual perceive that certain behaviors will lead to specified outcomes? (3) What values do individuals attach to these outcomes? The expectancy perspective implies the value of equity in the work situation, as well as the importance of consistent rewards; in fact, both equity and reinforcement theory have been viewed as special cases of expectancy theory. It also addresses the issue of individual differences and offers the opportunity for quantification of the various facets of motivation. Hence, expectancy theory, more than any other presented thus far, offers a comprehensive diagnostic tool.

Other process theories of motivation, such as reinforcement theory, goal-setting theory, and redesign of work, have also been found to be effective. Given the number of motivation theories available, which can be very perplexing, perhaps the best approach for the educator is to be situationally selective. Steers and Porter write, "In recent years . . . the notion of a multiple strategy using different approaches to motivation at one time or another depending upon the nature of the organization, its technology, its people, and its goals and priorities has come to be labeled a 'contingency approach' to management."[7]

Diagnostic Checklist

Here are some questions that might be addressed in assessing your institution's motivational process through the lens of structural functionalism, critical theory, and the Ignatian vision:

* Do the rewards satisfy the variety of individual needs?
* Are rewards both intrinsic and extrinsic?
* Are they applied equitably and consistently?
* Do individuals value the rewards they receive?
* Do they perceive that their efforts correlate with performance?
* Do individuals set goals as a source of motivation?
* Are the rewards and incentives effective in motivating desired behaviors?
* Does the rationale for motivation benefit both the institution and the individual?
* Is ethical behavior rewarded?

THE COMMUNICATION PROCESS

One of the perennial complaints of school personnel is a lack of communication between themselves and another segment of the school community, frequently the administration. If the transformational leader is to be effective, therefore, he or she must master the skill of effective communication.

Feedback is perhaps the most important aspect of the communications process. Feedback refers to an acknowledgement by the receiver that the message has been received; it provides the sender with information about the receiver's understanding of the message being sent.

Often, one-way communication occurs between administrators and their colleagues. Because of inherent power differences in their positions, administrators may give large quantities of information and directions to their faculty and staff without providing them the opportunity to show their understanding or accurate and clear receipt of the information. These managers often experience conflict between their role as authorities and a desire to be liked by their colleagues. Other administrators have relied on the use of written memoranda as a way of communicating with faculty and staff. In addition to the inherent lack of feedback involved in this method, the use of a single channel of communication also limits the effectiveness of communication. The proliferation of the use of e-mail has alleviated this problem somewhat by providing a relatively facile feedback mechanism. Of course, the misuse and over-use of e-mail presents its own set of problems.

Why do administrators sometimes not involve their faculty and staff in two-way communication? In some instances, administrators do not trust their colleagues to contribute effectively. In other situations, the lack of self-confidence on the part of the administrator makes him or her appear uninterested in others' opinions. Or, administrators are sure that their faculty and staff have the same goals as they do and, thus, feel that input from colleagues is not required or would not add anything of significance to the process. Of course, none of these attitudes is consistent with critical theory and the Ignatian vision. Encouraging feedback from others helps show them that you are concerned about them as individuals in ways that go beyond merely ensuring that they produce.

So-called subordinates also have a responsibility for encouraging two-way communication. While managers may attempt to protect their power positions, subordinates attempt to protect the image their supervisors hold of them. Frequently, for example, assistant superintendents withhold negative information about their departments for fear that it may reflect negatively on them. Or, they may fail to inform the superintendent about their needs and values. Other subordinates mistrust their superiors and so withhold information from them. Why do these situations arise? Some subordinates may assume that they and their supervisors have different goals and agendas. Others mistrust their supervisors because of past behavior. Still others lack persistence in seeking responses from their supervisors. Impressions of management, therefore, play a key role in whether individuals send in feedback. They may assess in what way asking for feedback will be interpreted and how the resulting information will affect each person's public image. In order for effective communication to take place, then, subordinates must show that they, too, are willing to build relationships with their supervisors. Thus, a culture of mutual trust and respect, of which we spoke earlier, is a requisite for effective communication.

What can individuals do to improve their communication in both formal and informal settings? There are at least two ways of improving communication effectiveness: creating a supportive communication climate using an assertive communication style and using active-listening techniques.

In communicating with their faculties and staffs, administrators know they must create a trusting and supportive environment. Creating such a climate has the objective of shifting from evaluation to problem solving and formation in communication. They must avoid making employees feel defensive, that is, threatened by the communication. They can create such an atmosphere in at least six ways:[8]

1. They use descriptive, rather than evaluative, speech and do not imply that the receiver needs to change. An administrator may describe teacher traits in terms of strengths and areas in need of further development, rather than describing them as weaknesses.
2. They take a problem-solving orientation, which implies a desire to collaborate in exploring a mutual problem, rather than to control or change the listener. An administrator can ask teachers what they hope to achieve in a lesson or for the academic year, rather than setting out a list of goals for them.
3. They are spontaneous, honest, and open rather than appearing to use strategy that involves ambiguous and multiple motivations. A superintendent might share with the school community the need for restructuring the possible areas of downsizing, rather than doing so surreptitiously.
4. They convey empathy for the feelings of their listeners, rather than appearing unconcerned or neutral about the listeners' welfare. They give reassurance that they are identifying with the listener's problems, rather than denying the legitimacy of the problems. When reviewing a union grievance with a teacher, the principal may indicate sensitivity to the teacher's position, even though the decision may ultimately go against the teacher.
5. They indicate that they feel equal rather than superior to the listener. Thus, they suggest that they will enter a shared relationship, not simply dominate the interaction. A college dean may come out from behind his or her desk and sit next to a colleague to indicate a relationship of equality.

6. Finally, they communicate that they will experiment with their own behavior and ideas, rather than be dogmatic about them. They do not give the impression that they know all the answers and need no help from anyone. An administrator can concede that he or she does not know if his or her suggestion will work, but ask the employee in question to "give it a try."

In addition, supportive communication emphasizes congruence between thoughts and feelings and communication. An individual who feels unappreciated by a supervisor, for example, must communicate that feeling to the supervisor, rather than deny it or communicate it inaccurately. Communication must also validate an individual's importance, uniqueness, and worth. Nondefensive communication recognizes the other person's existence; it recognizes the person's uniqueness as an individual, rather than treating him or her as a role or a job; it acknowledges the worth of the other person; it acknowledges the validity of the other person's perception of the world; and, it expresses a willingness to be involved with the other person, at least during the communication.

Interpersonal communication can be improved by encouraging individuals to communicate by using as complete a knowledge of themselves and others as possible. The Johari window provides an analytical tool that individuals can use to identify information that is available for use in communication. In the Johari window, information about an individual is represented along two dimensions: (1) information known and unknown by the self, and (2) information known and unknown by others.

Together these dimensions form a four-category representation of the individual. The open self is information known by the self and known by others. The blind self is information unknown by the self and known by others, such as others' perceptions of your behavior or attitudes. The concealed self is information known by you and unknown by others. Secrets we keep from others about ourselves fall into this category. Finally, the unconscious self is information that is unknown to the self and unknown to others. To ensure quality communication, in most cases an individual should communicate from his or her open self to another's open self and limit the amount of information concealed or in the blind spot. Guarded communication may be appropriate, however, if one party has violated trust in the past, if the parties have an adversarial relationship, if power and status differentials characterize the culture, if the relationship is transitory, or if the corporate culture does not support openness. This last criterion would, of course, not exist in an institution inspired by critical theory and the Ignatian vision.

Another approach is improving communication using an assertive communication style. An assertive style, which is honest, direct, and firm, is contrasted to an aggressive style at one extreme and a nonassertive style at the other. With this style a person expresses personal needs, opinions, and feelings in honest and direct ways and stands up for his or her rights without violating the other person's rights. Assertive behavior is reflected in the content and the nonverbal style of the message. The assertive delegator, for example, "is clear and direct when explaining work to subordinates, doesn't hover, and . . . criticizes fairly, objectively, and constructively."[9]

Consider the situation of a superintendent whose assistant has missed two important deadlines in the past month. How could she respond assertively? She might say to her assistant, "I know you missed the last two deadlines. Is there an explanation I should know about? It is important that you meet the next deadlines." Her assertive response can include the expression of anger, frustration, or disappointment, but is couched in terms that would allow for feedback to obtain the employee's explanation for the behavior. This distinguishes it from an aggressive style, which is inappropriate behavior.

We can further contrast the assertive approach to nonassertive and aggressive styles. Nonassertive communication describes behavior in which the sender does not stand up for personal rights and indicates that his or feelings are unimportant; the person may be hesitant, apologetic, or fearful. In the situation of a missed deadline, nonassertive behavior might involve saying nothing to your assistant, hoping the situation will not recur. Individuals act nonassertively because they may mistake assertion for aggression or nonassertion for politeness or being helpful; refuse to accept their personal rights and responsibilities; experience anxiety about the negative consequences of assertiveness; or lack assertiveness skills.[10]

Aggressive communication is standing up for an individual's rights without respecting the rights of the other person. Aggressive behavior attempts to dominate and control others by sounding accusing or superior. In the situation of the missed deadlines, an aggressive response might be. "You always miss deadlines. You're taking advantage of me and the situation. If you miss another deadline, disciplinary action will be taken." While such a response may result in the desired behavior in the short run, its long-term consequences likely will be dysfunctional, resulting in distrust between the individuals involved. Ultimately, such behavior will negatively affect productivity and will especially affect the submission of creative and innovative solutions offered to management by the employee. Finally, such behavior is inconsistent with the Ignatian vision.

Active listening, which requires understanding both the content and the intent of a message, is still another way of improving communication. It can be facilitated by paraphrasing, perception checking, and behavior description.

The receiver can paraphrase the message conveyed by the sender. For example, if the sender states, "I don't like the work I am doing," the receiver might paraphrase it as, "Are you saying that you are dissatisfied with the profession of education? Or are you dissatisfied with the grade that you teach? Or do you wish to be reassigned to another school?" Note that these ways of paraphrasing the original message suggest very different understandings of the original statement. The sender, upon receiving this feedback from the receiver, can then clarify his or her meaning.

Alternatively, the receiver may perception-check, that is, describe what he or she perceives as the sender's inner state at the time of communication to check his or her understanding of the message. For example, if the sender states, "I don't like the work I am doing," the receiver might check his or her perception of the statement by asking, "Are you dissatisfied with the way you are being treated, or are you dissatisfied with me as a supervisor?" Note that answers to these two questions will identify different feelings.

A third way of checking communication is through behavior description. Here the individual reports specific, observable actions of others without making accusations or generalizations about their motives, personalities, or characteristics. Similarly, descriptions of feelings, where the individual specifies or identifies feelings by name, analogy, or some other verbal representation, can increase active listening. For example, to help others understand you as a person, you should describe what others did that affects you personally or as a group member. Then, you can let others know as clearly and unambiguously as possible what you are feeling.

Moving beyond individual communication, let us now address the communication networks that are prevalent in many schools. Communication is embedded in all school structures. In the traditional, classical or bureaucratic model, formal communication channels, or networks, traverse the institution through the hierarchy of authority. In most academic institutions there are formal communication channels and every member of the institution reports to someone. For instance, curriculum directors report to the assistant superintendent for instruction, who, with the assistant superintendent for finance, reports to the superintendent. The lines of communication from the superintendent to the teachers go through several hierarchical levels. This is reasonably short and direct for a large school district.

With all organizations, formal restrictions on the communication process are apparent. "Making certain to go through proper channels" and "following the chain of command" are two common expressions that are a reflection of communication in organizations. Three characteristics of school bureaucracies seem particularly critical in communication: centralization in the hierarchy, the organization's shape or configuration, and the level of information technology.[11]

The degree that authority is not delegated but concentrated in a single source in the organization is important to the effectiveness of communication systems. In centralized schools, a few positions in the structure have most of the information-obtaining ability. For example, the superintendent and the two assistant superintendents in our above illustration would gather most of the information for the formal system of communication. If the district is decentralized or loosely coupled, however, the information-obtaining potential is more or less spread across all of the positions. Research examining the different information-obtaining abilities supports the finding that centralized structures are more efficient communicators when the problems and tasks are relatively simple and straightforward. When the problems and tasks become more complex, however, decentralized hierarchies appear to be more efficient. We would argue that because the process of education is by nature complex, communication in an educational setting would be facilitated by a more decentralized structure (social-systems or open-system models).

The number of hierarchical levels, or tallness versus flatness, of the school organization also affects the communication process. Hierarchical levels and size are structural characteristics that are commonly associated with the shape of an organization. A school district with five levels differs from systems with more or fewer levels in its ability to communicate across levels and from top to bottom. The number of levels can be seen as the distance a message must travel. As the distance increases, the chance of message distortion increases, and the satisfaction with the quality and quantity of communication decreases. Teachers will generally express less satisfaction with messages from superintendents than from principals. In addition, organizational size is negatively related to communication quality; as the district becomes larger, communication becomes more impersonal or formal, and quality declines. This is part of the reason that the subdividing of large school districts into charter schools and "houses" within schools is proliferating. For communication and other purposes, smaller is sometimes better.

To overcome some of the problems inherent in the classical structure of most organizations, including schools, matrix, or mixed, designs have evolved to improve mechanisms of lateral communication and information flow across the organization.

The matrix organization, originally developed in the aerospace industry and is characterized by a dual authority system. There are usually functional and program or product-line managers, both reporting to a common superior and both exercising authority over workers within the matrix. Typically, a matrix organization is particularly useful in highly specialized technological areas that focus on innovation. But that certainly does not preclude its use in those educational settings where creativity is fostered. The matrix design allows program managers to interact directly with the environment vis-à-vis new developments. Usually each program requires a multidisciplinary team approach; the matrix structure facilitates the coordination of the team and allows team members to contribute their special expertise.

The use of matrix design in education is not very common, but it is a viable way of organizing when communication needs to occur outside the "proper channels." The popularity of interdisciplinary and multicultural courses and programs in education has caused an increased interest in the matrix design. Many high schools and colleges are informally organized in a matrix design. It would most likely serve these institutions well to consider matrix design as a formal organizational structure, especially in cases when communication problems are evident.

Technology also appears to have a significant effect on organizational communication, although that effect remains somewhat speculative. Compared to other organizations, schools, and even colleges, have relatively low levels of technology. However, as communication technology becomes more sophisticated in schools, its use will dramatically alter the communication that takes place in both the formal and informal networks.

We are living in a creative and dynamic era that is producing fundamental changes, as is apparent in such advances as computer networks, electronic mail, computer conferences, communication satellites, data-handling devices, and the various forms of distance education. Until recently, electronic information exchange has largely been adapted to convey voice, vision, text, and graphics as distinct and separate types of communication. During the next few years, simultaneous and instantaneous transmission of voice, vision, text, and graphics to many locations will be common. Even imagining these technologies together with the geographic distribution of participants does not adequately capture the differences between these and traditional media. Consequently, the potential influence of such technologies on all aspects of communication in schools is probably underestimated.

Next, we need to make a distinction between internal and external communication and the appropriate communication network for each. We have suggested that for internal communication purposes, a loosely structured communication network would be most effective. Although the principles of effective communication still prevail when dealing with the outside community, some nuances need to be stressed. Perhaps the most important aspect of communication that needs to be considered when dealing with the public is the uniformity of the message. The message must be clear and consistent and must emanate from a single source. In these cases, the chain of command and channels of communication need to be well defined and structured along the lines of the classical model. It is imperative that the school "speak with one voice."

Someone in the school district should be designated as the clearing-house for all external communication. This individual, or office, should review all external communication for clarity and accuracy, and school personnel should be keenly aware of the school's policy with regard to external communication. Examples abound of the communications nightmares caused by organizations that did not speak with one voice to external publics. Thus, although a more loosely structured communication system is very appropriate for internal communication, a more tightly structured one is necessary for effective external communication.

An anecdote may be appropriate here. A foreign-born plumber in New York once wrote to the Bureau of Standards that he found hydrochloric acid fine for cleaning drains, and he asked if they agreed. Washington replied, "The efficacy of hydrochloric acid is indisputable, but the chlorine residue is incompatible with metallic permanence." The plumber wrote back that he was mighty glad the bureau agreed with him.

Considerably alarmed, the Bureau replied a second time: "We cannot assume responsibility for the production of toxic and noxious residues with hydrochloric acid and suggest that you use an alternative procedure." The plumber was happy to learn that the Bureau still agreed with him. Whereupon Washington wrote, "Don't use hydrochloric acid; it eats the hell out of pipes."

Communicating with ease and clarity is no simple task. There are, however, various theories about how it can be most effectively carried out. Classical theory, social-systems theory, and open-system theory all incorporate a perspective toward the communication process, that is, toward who should say what through which channel to whom and to what effect. Classical theory stresses that the communication process exists to facilitate the manager's command and control over the employees in a formal, hierarchical, and downwardly directed manner. The purpose is to increase efficiency and productivity.

The social-systems orientation suggests that to be effective, communication has to be two-way and that the meaning of the message is as much to be found in the psychological makeup of the receiver as it is in the sender's intent. The channels can be informal, as well as formal, and include anyone who has an interest in a particular subject.

The open-system orientation emphasizes the communication process working toward drawing the various subsystems of an organization into a collaborating whole, as in a matrix system of communication. Also, drawing the organization's actions into a close fit with the needs of its environment is an essential outcome of the process. This orientation emphasizes that between senders and receivers, the communication process must penetrate social-class differences, cultural values, time orientations, and ethnocentrism of all types. In this way, open-system communications encompasses the spirit of critical theory and the Ignatian vision.

None of the conceptual frameworks, by itself, escapes the barriers to communication. The story of the plumber illustrates the problems of message coding, decoding, and transmission. We have suggested that in order for communication to be effective, we should adapt the process to the situation. We have suggested that when communicating with the outside community, a structured process may be appropriate, while when communicating with the inside community, a less structured process may be appropriate. This situational approach is in concert with one of the underlying themes of this book, that whether we are speaking about organizational structure, leadership, motivation, or communication, we need to adapt the approach or model to the situation in which we find ourselves. Thus, the structural-functionalist organizational models need to be adapted to the situation, while the principles of critical theory and the Ignatian vision are applicable no matter what the situation.

Diagnostic Checklist

Here are some questions than can be addressed in assessing your institution's communication process through the lens of structural functionalism, critical theory, and the Ignatian vision:

- How effective is the communication process at your institution?
- What barriers to communication exist?
- Is the correct communication structure utilized in a given situation?
- Does communication include feedback, where appropriate?
- Is there a climate of mutual trust and respect to facilitate the communication process?
- Are active listening and other techniques that improve communication being used?

- Do individuals use assertive, rather than nonassertive or aggressive, communication styles?
- Are individuals communicating from the open self?

CONFLICT MANAGEMENT

A few years ago, I invited Dr. Janet Baker, a well-known authority on conflict, to address a group of principals at a Principals' Academy offered at Saint Joseph's University in Philadelphia. We introduced Dr. Baker's topic as conflict resolution. Upon taking the podium, Dr. Baker quickly corrected us and said that she was there to talk about conflict management, not conflict resolution: "If your goal as a principal is to resolve all conflict, you will be doomed to frustration and failure," she said. "The best that you can hope for is to manage conflict."

Conflict is the result of incongruent or incompatible potential-influence relationships between and within individuals, groups, or organizations. Conflict can be public or private, formal or informal, rational or nonrational. The likelihood of conflict increases when parties have the chance to interact, when the parties see their interests as incompatible, and when one or both parties sees some utility in engaging in conflict to resolve incompatibility.

Conflict most commonly results from four circumstances. First, when mutually exclusive goals or values actually exist or are perceived to exist by the groups involved, conflict can occur. In the collective bargaining process, for example, the teachers' union may perceive the administration's goals as in conflict with those of the teachers. Second, behavior designed to defeat, reduce, or suppress the opponent may cause conflict. Again, union and management have historically experienced conflict for this reason. Third, groups that face each other with mutually opposing actions and counteractions cause conflict. For example, if the second-grade teacher does not follow the curriculum, the third-grade teacher will be affected because the students will not have been properly prepared. Finally, if each group attempts to create a relatively favored position, conflict may occur. If the English department attempts to show the administration that it is superior to the other departments by demonstrating the others' ineptness, conflict occurs.

Conflict can have functional or dysfunctional outcomes. Whether conflict takes a constructive or destructive course is influenced by the sociocultural context in which the conflict occurs because differences tend to exaggerate barriers and reduce the likelihood of conflict resolution. The issues involved will also affect the likely outcomes. Whether the parties have cooperative, individualistic, or competitive orientations toward conflict will affect the outcomes as well. Obviously, those with cooperative attitudes are more likely to seek a functional outcome. The characteristics of the conflicting parties also affect conflict behavior. Finally, misjudgments and misperceptions contribute to dysfunctional conflict.

Effective managers learn how to create functional conflict and manage dysfunctional conflict. They develop and practice techniques for diagnosing the causes and nature of conflict and transforming it into a productive force in the organization. Many universities, for example, have a healthy competition among their schools for recruitment of the most qualified students.

Some conflict is beneficial. It can encourage organizational innovation, creativity, and adaptation. We will see later that at least a low level of conflict is needed to spur on needed change. For example, a number of nonpublic-school systems, and even some public-school systems, allow schools within the system to compete for the same students. This open-enrollment policy often spawns innovation in marketing techniques, and more importantly, in curricula and programs. In these cases, conflict can result in more worker enthusiasm and better decisions. Can you think of a situation where such positive outcomes occurred? Perhaps during a disagreement with a colleague you came to hold a different perspective on an issue or learned that your own perceptions or information had been inaccurate. Finally, in order to generate and implement the reforms suggested by critical theory and the Ignatian vision, oftentimes a sense of urgency or tension must exist.

On the other hand, conflict can be viewed as dysfunctional for organizations. It can reduce productivity, decrease morale, cause overwhelming dissatisfaction, and increase tension and stress in the organization. It can arouse anxiety in individuals, increase the tension in an organizational system and its subsystems, and lower satisfaction. In addition, some people, often the losers in a competitive situation, feel defeated and demeaned. As the distance between people increases, a climate of mistrust and suspicion may arise. Individuals or groups may focus more narrowly on their own interests, preventing the development of teamwork. Production and satisfaction may decline; turnover and absenteeism may increase. Diagnosing the location and type of conflict, as described next, is a first step in managing conflict so that it results in functional outcomes.

Administrators may encourage individuals or groups to use at least five behaviors or strategies for dealing with conflict: (1) avoidance, (2) accommodation, (3) compromise, (4) forcing, and (5) collaboration. These differ in the extent to which they satisfy a party's own and the other party's concerns. For example, a person or group that uses an avoiding mode is unassertive in satisfying their own concerns and uncooperative in satisfying others' concerns. In contrast, a person or group that uses a collaborating mode is assertive and cooperative.

Each style is appropriate to different situations that individuals or groups face in organizations. Once again, the underlying theme of contingency theory applies; that is, there is rarely one single approach that is applicable at all times in all situations. Rather, the effective model or approach will change depending on the situation. What does remain constant, however, is the applicability of the principles of critical theory and the Ignatian vision.

The behavior an individual or group chooses depends, therefore, on that party's experiences in dealing with conflict, his or her own personal disposition in interpersonal relations, and the specific elements of a particular conflict episode.

The first conflict-management style of which I will speak is that of avoidance. Individuals or groups may withdraw from a conflict situation. They act to satisfy neither their own or the other party's concerns. Avoidance works best when individuals or groups face trivial or tangential issues, when they have little chance of satisfying their personal concerns, when conflict resolution will likely result in significant disruption, or when others can resolve the conflict more effectively. If two secretaries in the secretarial pool, for example, have an argument, the most appropriate strategy for managing the conflict may be avoidance. Let the secretaries resolve the conflict in their own way. It is like the proverbial story of the next-door neighbors whose children get into an argument, and the adults try to intervene on behalf of their respective children. The adults end up enemies for life, and the children begin playing with each other again within the hour.

Once leaders decide that avoidance is not the appropriate conflict-management style, they must then decide proactively which remaining style would be most effective in resolving the conflict. Individuals or groups who use accommodation demonstrate a willingness to cooperate in satisfying others' concerns, while at the same time acting unassertively in meeting their own. Accommodating individuals often smooth over conflict. This mode builds social credits for later issues, results in harmony and stability, and satisfies others. An assistant principal may capitulate on a disagreement with the principal over a minor matter in hopes that he or she can prevail on a larger issue in the future; thus, he or she is attempting to build political capital for later use.

The compromise mode represents an intermediate behavior between the assertiveness and cooperation dimensions. It can include sharing positions, but not moving to the extremes of assertiveness or cooperation. Hence, it often does not maximize the satisfaction of both parties. This style works well when goals are important, but not sufficiently important for the individual or group to be more assertive, when the two parties have equal power, or when significant time pressure exists. For example, if two grade partners disagree over which supplementary materials should be used for a certain lesson, they may compromise and use some of each teacher's suggestion.

Using the forcing mode, a party tries to satisfy his or her own concerns while showing an unwillingness to satisfy the other's concerns to even a minimal degree. This strategy works well in emergencies, on issues calling for unpopular actions, and in cases when one party is correct in its position or has much greater power. For example, if a child threatens to commit suicide, the principal may wish to inform the parents immediately, and the guidance counselor may wish to keep the information confidential. If the principal arbitrarily informs the parents, he or she is using a forcing behavior. Critical theory and the Ignatian vision would prompt us to use this conflict-management style very infrequently.

The collaboration mode emphasizes problem solving with a goal of maximizing satisfaction for both parties. It means seeing conflict as natural, showing trust and honesty toward others, and encouraging the airing of every person's attitudes and feelings. Each party exerts both assertive and cooperative behavior. Parties can use it when their objectives are to learn, to use information from diverse sources, and to find an integrative solution. If the teachers' union and the school board establish a mutually satisfactory way of working together, they are taking a collaborative, or problem-solving, approach to resolving or avoiding conflict. Unfortunately, the history of labor-management relations has been adversarial, featuring forcing, compromising, and accommodating behavior, rather than collaborative behavior. A good rule of thumb in managing conflicts is to begin with a collaborative style, while using the other modes only when collaboration has not brought about the desired results.

Diagnostic Checklist

Here are some questions that can be addressed in assessing your institution's conflict-management process through the lens of structural functionalism, critical theory, and the Ignatian vision:

- Is the conflict in the institution functional or dysfunctional?
- Are mechanisms for effectively managing conflict and stress present?
- Do the mechanisms reflect the situational nature of conflict management?
- Are avoidance, compromise, competition, accommodation, and collaboration utilized in the appropriate situations?
- Is the competition, or forcing, style used sparingly or routinely?
- Is collaboration the preferred means of conflict management?
- Is the care of the individual an important impetus for conflict management?
- Are cultural differences and values considered in the conflict-management process?

THE DECISION-MAKING PROCESS

According to Vroom and Yetton, the two most important aspects of a decision are its quality and its acceptance.[12] A good-quality decision brings about the desired result while meeting relevant criteria and constraints. The quality of the decision depends in part on the level of the decision maker's technical or task skills, interpersonal or leadership skills, and decision-making skills. Technical or task skills refer to the individual's knowledge of the particular area in which the decision is being made. Interpersonal or leadership skills relate to the way individuals lead, communicate with, motivate, and influence others. Decision-making skills are the basic abilities to perform the components of the decision-making process, including situational analysis, objective setting, and generation, evaluation, and selection of alternatives, as discussed later in this chapter. The other important factor, acceptance, is the extent to which acceptance or commitment on the part of subordinates is crucial to the effective implementation ot the decision. In addition to quality and acceptance, another factor that we would espouse in light of our commitment to critical theory and the Ignatian vision would be the ethics or morality of the decision.

The relationship of quality to acceptance is critical in determining the appropriate decision-making strategy. For example, if a new legal procedure is passed regarding the treatment of students with disabilities, and the administrator has to decide if and how it should be placed in the faculty and student handbook, the quality of the decision will be more important than the acceptance. Therefore, Vroom and Yetton would suggest that the appropriate decision style is command. In other words, the leader makes the decision by him- or herself. On the other hand, if acceptance is more important than quality, as in the development of a new teacher-evaluation instrument, the proper decision style would be consensus.

If both the quality and acceptance are of equal importance, as in whether to adopt a whole-language approach to reading, consultation or group decision making would be the appropriate style. Finally, if neither the quality nor the acceptance is important, such as deciding what color to paint the school lockers, convenience would be the applicable style. Simply find out what color paint you have available in the district warehouse.

While the literature on administrative and organizational theory are in agreement about the two most important factors to be considered in determining the decision style that will produce the most effective decisions, there is far less agreement about the importance of the third factor, ethical fairness and justice. Consider, for example, a disastrous decline in standardized test scores in one of the high schools in a school district. Top administrators are faced with deciding whether to admit the facts and risk public outrage and the possible transfer of significant numbers of students or to ignore the situation and hope that it is not detected.

Administrators and staff can assess whether the decisions they make are ethical by applying personal moral codes or their society's code of values. They can apply philosophical views of ethical behavior, or they can assess the potential harmful consequences of behaviors to certain constituencies. One way of thinking about ethical decision making suggests that a person who makes a moral decision must first recognize the moral issue of whether a person's actions can hurt or help others; second, make a moral judgment; third, decide to attach greater priority to moral concerns than to financial or other material concerns; and finally, act on the moral concerns of the situation by engaging in moral behaviors.[13]

The decision-making processes described thus far can apply to decisions made by individuals or groups. Yet, group decision making brings different resources to the task than does individual decision making. When a group makes a decision, a synergy occurs that causes the group decision to be better than the sum of the individual decisions. The involvement of more than one individual brings additional knowledge and skills to the decision, and it tends to result in higher-quality decisions. However, the same caveat holds true for decision making as with other processes discussed earlier; that is, decision making is situational, and the idiosyncrasies of the moment dictate the decision-making approach to be taken. For example, if the school building is on fire, participative decision making is not appropriate.

In most cases, using a rational, sequential decision-making process, often called the rational decision-making process, increases the likelihood that a high-quality, accepted, ethical decision will result. It involves the six steps of situational analysis, objective setting, generation of alternatives, evaluation of alternatives, making of the decision, and evaluation of the decision. Let us look at these steps in turn, using a case study where a school district is forced to restructure itself due to declining enrollments.

Decision making first involves the recognition that there is a problem to be solved or a decision to be made, followed by exploration and classification of the decision situation.[14] Decision making then requires asking such questions as what are the key elements of the situation? What constraints affect the decision? What resources are available? How will the leader answer these questions? The key elements include, among others, such issues as the past performance of various schools and faculties, the academic reputation of the schools and the school district, the projected demographic information, the profit margin in each school, any special needs in certain neighborhoods, the overhead costs for each school, and contractual issues. The leader must consider his or her previous experience in effecting restructuring and how the various components of the school community reacted to his or her efforts. The leader must then assess whether approaches which were successful in the past can be effective in the new situation.

Constraints on the decision will include the state laws regarding faculty downsizing, as well as the local labor-agreement constraints. While limitations on resources and constraints such as those mentioned can be debilitating, they can also generate creative alternatives. For example, if simply laying people off is restricted, one can offer early retirement and voluntary severance packages to achieve the rightsizing objectives. From this situational analysis, the decision maker begins to formulate the issues to be addressed.

The way the decision makers frame the problem has a significant impact on its ultimate resolution. Subsequent steps may differ, for example, if the leader frames the problems as cost reduction, downsizing, or an opportunity to serve the constituencies in a more effective and efficient way that will ensure the long-range future of the school district. Errors in problem definition may be hard to identify and even harder to correct. The decision maker should carefully identify the goals and objectives that the decision must accomplish and specify the criteria that will be used to assess its quality, acceptance, and ethical appropriateness. The accomplishment of these goals and objectives serves as one measure of the effectiveness of the decision and the decision-making process.[15]

Often, decision makers err at this step by confusing action plans with objectives. Decision makers must first set their goals and, then, determine ways of accomplishing them. For example, offering all eligible teachers early retirement is one way of accomplishing the goal of rightsizing. In this case, the early retirement program is not the goal, but a means to achieving a goal.

When possible, decision makers should establish objectives that specify observable and measurable results. Certainly, reducing absenteeism and costs or increasing standardized test scores by a specified percentage or amount are objectives that are observable and measurable. Objectives related to employee attitudes, such as satisfaction, commitment, or involvement, may be more difficult to measure and observe. Still, skillful crafting of the objectives by the decision maker can meet the need for quantifiable and observable results even in these difficult-to-measure instances.

The decision maker specifies a set of realistic and potentially acceptable solutions to the problem or numerous ways of meeting the objectives specified earlier as part of the searching-for-alternatives phase. What alternatives are available in that downsizing example? The leader can close no schools, but offer early retirement incentives to decrease costs; close one or two schools and lay off a number of teachers; reduce an administrative layer; increase the class sizes and lay off a number of teachers; or effect efficiencies throughout the school system in both academic and nonacademic areas. Techniques for generating alternatives are described later in this chapter.

The decision maker next appraises each alternative. Criteria for evaluation include the alternative's feasibility, cost, and reliability. In addition, the decision maker must assess the risks involved and the likelihood of certain outcomes for each alternative. What other criteria might be used in evaluating the alternatives? For example, what will the taxpayers think of the alternatives? What about the school board? Will local or national politicians prefer one alternative to another? Are there advocacy groups to consider? All of these factors and more need to be considered before making a decision.

Quantifying the alternatives can systematize their evaluation, dramatizing the difference among them, and even improving the quality of decision making. For example, we might score each of the alternatives on its feasibility, cost, potentially adverse consequences, and probability of success. Summing the scores of each alternative would allow us to rank-order them and, ultimately, select the highest one. The process assumes that the criteria are equally weighted, that the numerical values are exact, and that ranks alone are sufficient to provide the best choice. More sophisticated statistical treatment can also be used for such an evaluation. Obviously, this approach to quantifying the evaluation of alternatives is highly subjective because the decision maker's rating of each criterion is incorporated into the overall evaluation. Recent research suggests that decision makers evaluate alternatives using a compatibility test. In decision making, which can be either intuitive or deliberative, the decision maker compares each alternative with a set of standards, such as values, moral, beliefs, goals, and plans, called images. The decision maker rejects incompatible alternatives and adds compatible ones to the set of feasible alternatives.

The next step in the process is making the decision. Ideally, a decision maker should select the optimal, or best, alternative. Note, however, that the decision maker's knowledge, abilities, and motivation will affect the choice. In addition, each alternative has disadvantages, as well as advantages. If the cost criterion outweighs all others, then closing schools and laying off teachers and staff would be the best solution. If a moderate cost reduction, for which the leader should lobby, is acceptable and a low likelihood of adverse consequences is desired, then offering early retirement or some other less drastic alternative may be acceptable. Of course, the moral and ethical implications of the various alternatives need to be considered through the dual lenses of critical theory and the Ignatian vision.

Next comes the evaluation of the decision. Review of the decision is an essential step in effective decision making. Too often, selecting an alternative and reaching a decision make up the final step. Individuals must pause and check their decisions and the process that led to them as one way of increasing their effectiveness. Where possible, the decision maker might check his or her thinking with another person or group. Together they can evaluate the planned implementation of the decision by assessing its likely outcomes and comparing them to the objectives set earlier. Evaluation performed after implementation is part of management control and may call for corrective action and follow-up.

The next question one might logically ask is how can decision makers overcome barriers, reduce biases, and make more effective decisions? There are at least three techniques that can improve decision making: (1) brainstorming, (2) the nominal group technique, and (3) the Delphi technique. We address each of these techniques in detail in the next chapter, but for now we can summarize them.

Most of us are familiar with brainstorming. Groups or individuals use brainstorming when creativity is needed to generate alternatives for consideration in decision making. In brainstorming, as many alternatives as possible are listed without a simultaneous evaluation of the feasibility of any one. The use of this technique is limited, however, to less complex decisions.

The nominal group technique is a structured group meeting that helps resolve differences in group opinion by having individuals generate and rank-order a series of ideas in the problem-exploration, alternative-generation, or choice-making stage of group decision making. It has the advantage of being effective with more complex decision making.

The Delphi technique can be used in making complex decisions. It involves four phases: (1) exploration of the subject by individuals, (2) reaching an understanding of the group's view of the issues, (3) sharing and evaluation of any reasons for differences, and (4) final evaluation of all information. In the conventional Delphi, a small group designs a questionnaire, which is completed by a larger respondent group. The results are then tabulated and used in developing a revised questionnaire, which is again completed by the larger group. Thus, the results of the original polling are fed back to the respondent group to use in subsequent responses. This procedure is repeated until the issues are narrowed, responses are focused, or consensus is reached.

Diagnostic Checklist

Here are some questions that can be addressed in assessing your institution's decision-making process through the lens of structural functionalism, critical theory, and the Ignatian vision:

- Do organizational members make high-quality, accepted, and ethical decisions?
- Do decision makers follow the basic rational process of decision making?
- Is the group appropriately involved in decision making?

- What barriers to effective decision making exist?
- What techniques are being used to overcome these barriers?
- What techniques are being used to improve decision making?
- Is participative decision making being used whenever possible?
- Are all components of the school community given opportunities for equitable input in decision making?
- Is the input from certain constituencies being marginalized?

POWER DISTRIBUTION

Charlotte Burton is the fictitious new principal of Springfield High School. She met Ben Wilson, the teacher union representative, on her first day at the school. The two educators were strong-willed individuals who had reached their respective positions by aggressively pursuing their professional goals. They were both intent on showing the other who was boss.

The above scenario is not unlike many that occur in educational institutions of all levels. This situation reflects the exercise of power in an organization. Power is the potential or actual ability to influence others in a desired direction. An individual, group, or other social unit has power if it controls information, knowledge, or resources desired by another individual, group, or social unit. The presence of power and the distribution of power are important issues to critical theorists. They are concerned that society has developed a power structure that perpetuates the dominant culture to the detriment of the minority culture. This concept is often called hegemony.

Who has the power in the situation described at Springfield High School? Recognizing, using, and dealing with power differences is implicit in negotiation, which is a process for reconciling different, often incompatible, interests among interdependent parties. At Springfield High School, both Charlotte Burton and Ben Wilson have power. How well each of them uses his or her power and negotiation skills will determine their effectiveness.

Organizational researchers have increasingly cited the value of identifying and using power behavior to improve individual and organizational performance, even calling its development and use "the central executive function."[16] Theorists and practitioners have transformed an early view of power, which considered it evil and as mainly stemming from coercion, into a model of viable political action in organizations. Yet, while functional and advantageous in many situations, power behavior can create conflict, which frequently is dysfunctional for the organization.

Different individuals and groups within and outside the organization can exert power. For example, individual employees, including top and middle management, technical specialists, support staff, and other nonmanagerial employees can influence the actions an organization takes to reach its goals.[17] Thus, there are many sources of power. The three that we will discuss here include position power, personal power, and information or resource power.

In possessing position power, administrators can exert influence over others simply because of the authority associated with their jobs. It results in subordinates obeying the instructions given by a principal, for example, simply by virtue of the position that he or she holds. In education, the union contract and tenure mitigate the principal's position power to a significant degree. Thus, it is inappropriate to rely on position as the only source of power. One study showed, for example, that as a supervisor's position power increased, a subordinate's compliance increased, but his or her satisfaction with the supervision decreased.[18] So in the long run, the abuse of position power can have diminishing returns.

Personal power is based on the knowledge or personality of an individual that allows him or her to influence the behavior of others. An individual who has unique or special knowledge, skills, and experience may use this expertise as a source of influence and as a way of building personal power. When the use of computers first made its impact on schools, for example, the "computer guru" on the faculty oftentimes wielded personal power based on special knowledge and skills. As schools and other organizations have become increasingly technology-oriented, technical support staff have acquired increased power and influence.

Information or resource power provides a third major source of influence. This differs from expert power in its greater transience. Expertise is more permanent than information-based power. For example, the first individuals to learn to use a new computer system may initially derive their power from having information that others do not possess, but if their power persists after even the average teacher becomes computer literate, they have developed personal power based on expertise.

Power may also come from the control of scarce resources, such as money, materials, staff, or information. In a school setting, the business manager often has this type of power. Even the audiovisual director can have this type of power if there is a greater demand than supply of these types of resources in a school.

Recent research suggests that individuals can increase their own power by sharing power with others. Administrators can facilitate such sharing by helping colleagues to understand and tap into the sources of power described above. They can also give them empowering information, such as providing emotional support or affirmation, serving as a role model, and facilitating the successful accomplishment of a task. Other strategies for the empowering process for administrators include providing a positive emotional atmosphere, rewarding staff achievements in visible and personal ways, expressing confidence in subordinates' abilities, fostering initiative and responsibility, and building on success.

Discussing the empowering of others leads us to a discussion of the legitimate or ethical use of power in organizations. Certainly, if the use of power is manipulative and autocratic, it raises questions about the ethics of power. The abuse of power is evident not only in politics and business, but also in schools and school districts across the nation. But the use of power, so long as it does not abuse the rights of others, has been encouraged in organizations. It both helps administrators attain institutional goals and facilitates their own and others' achievements and expedites effective functioning in the workplace. Power viewed in this way is an essential part of effective administration and leadership.

Administrators must establish guidelines for the ethical use of power in their organizations. They and other organizational members must emphasize its contribution to organizational effectiveness and control its abuses. Ensuring that the rights of all organizational members are guaranteed is one criterion for its ethical use. This is especially appropriate in institutions that are not unionized, where the employee handbook should outline employee rights in a way similar to that of a labor agreement.

Another concern is the equitable distribution of power among individuals and groups. Leaders must be particularly attuned to the needs of those individuals or groups that are systematically marginalized by our society. Leaders need to examine the power implications of their decisions constantly. Even decisions that on the surface do not seem to have power-distribution implications may upon further analysis have immense implications for perpetuating the dominant culture. An example is a decision about homogenous versus heterogeneous grouping. Whether to track students according to ability is usually determined by considering the advantages and disadvantages to the students and the teachers. However, the manner in which such a policy impacts the sustenance of the dominant culture rarely enters the decision-making process. As practitioners of critical theory and the Ignatian vision, the social impact and the power implications of such decisions must be examined closely.

Perhaps nowhere is the importance of power distribution more critical than in the negotiation process. Negotiation is a process by which two or more parties attempt to reach an agreement that is acceptable to both parties about issues on which they disagree. Negotiations typically have four key elements. First, the two parties demonstrate some degree of interdependence. Second, some perceived conflict exists between the parties involved in the negotiations. Third, the two parties have the potential to participate in opportunistic interaction. Therefore, each party tries to influence the other through various negotiating strategies. Each party cares about and pursues its own interests by trying to influence decisions to its advantage. Finally, the possibility of agreement exists.

There are basically two bargaining paradigms in current use: distributive bargaining, which takes an adversarial or win-lose approach, and integrative bargaining, which takes a problem solving or win-win approach.[19]

The classical view considers bargaining as a win-lose situation, where one party's gain is the other party's loss. Known also as a zero-sum type of negotiation, because the gain of one party equals the loss of the other and, hence, the net is zero, this approach characterizes the great majority of the negotiations taking place in educational settings today.

Recent research, let alone the Ignatian vision, encourages negotiators to transform the bargaining into a win-win situation. Here both parties gain as a result of the negotiations. Known also as a positive-sum type of negotiation, because the gains of each party yield a positive sum, this approach has recently characterized the negotiations in a few school districts, especially those that have had a history of strikes and are looking for an alternative to the classical mode of collective bargaining.

Diagnostic Checklist

Here are some questions that can be addressed in assessing your institution's equitable distribution of power through the lens of structural functionalism, critical theory, and the Ignatian vision:

- Who has the power in the organization?
- From what sources does the power emanate?
- Is the power appropriately shared?
- Does the negotiation process tend to be distributive or integrative?
- Is empowerment taking place on a routine basis?
- Are distribution-of-power implications being considered in the decision-making process?
- Are the social implications of the distribution of power being considered?

THE STRATEGIC-PLANNING PROCESS

The strategic-planning process should be understood as a dynamic ebb and flow of events in the life of an educational institution. The so-called chaos theory tells us that life is a process, constantly changing and evolving. Therefore, it should not be surprising to see that some of the best-laid plans become obsolete before they see the light of day. Mirror Lake, for example, is slowly drying up and evolving into a meadow. If you were planning strategically for the future, you would do well to buy your grandchild a kite, rather than a boat, if he or she lived near Mirror Lake.

The morale of the story, therefore, is to plan for the unexpected, as well as the expected. Even though your school system may currently be prosperous and healthy, the only way to sustain this success is to plan for the possibility of difficult times. How do we know that the unexpected will eventually occur? One need only look at history.

What prevents us from planning accurately is our paradigm for how things are. We want to find order when the reality is chaos. We like to think that events occur in a linear way. This is how we have been trained. Positivistic theory leads us to believe that we can accurately predict outcomes. The reality is that events occur in a sporadic and unpredictable way. Our mission, then, is to find order in this apparent chaos. Thus, we must see our plans as constantly evolving and changing. The process is continuing. The plans themselves change so frequently that they are of limited value. As Dwight Eisenhower aptly pointed out, "Planning is all, but plans are nothing." The primacy of the planning process over the plan itself is a notion that the astute administrator will constantly keep in mind.

So let us look at the planning process. Strategic planning is a process that was first developed and refined in business and industry, but has been adopted by a variety of educational institutions throughout the nation. In some states, the process is mandated for all publicly funded educational institutions. Strategic planning begins with the development of a mission or vision statement. Goals and objectives are derived from the mission, and strategies are developed for achieving them. Although one may be built into existing structure, it is common practice to create a task force composed of representatives from all levels of the organization that is responsible for planning and making decisions. The process must look to the future.

The process of developing a mission statement involves establishing a strong group consensus about the unique purposes of the educational institution and its place in the community that it serves. The process of developing the mission will set the tone for all further planning activity. Most often, educational institutions have an existing mission. However, the planning process should not begin until there is broad acceptance of the mission. Many times the mission needs to be revised to adapt to current realities before the process can continue.

The mission statement, then, must be developed through discussion among the various constituencies that make up the school community, must be an outgrowth of a discussion of unique institutional purposes, and must reflect the unique character of the institution. The educational vision of the institution is derived from the mission statement. It is often a concise summary of the mission.

The institution should next develop a set of goals that it deems appropriate to the accomplishment of its mission. Goals are more specific and give direction to the action that needs to take place to achieve them. The goals should be expressed in terms that promote easy assessment.

It should be clear to an objective observer whether they have been achieved. Thus, the goals should be behavioral; that is, they should be measurable, hold someone accountable for their attainment, and provide a timeline for their completion. Hopefully, the mission and goals of the institution will reflect the values and ideals of critical theory and the Ignatian vision.

The planning process is completed by operationalizing or implementing the plan, evaluating its effectiveness, and institutionalizing it by making it part of the institution's identity or character.

Diagnostic Checklist

Here are some questions that can be addressed in assessing your institution's planning process through the lens of structural functionalism, critical theory, and the Ignatian vision:

- Does a mission statement exist?
- Does a vision statement exist?
- Does the mission reflect the values and ideals of critical theory and the Ignatian vision?
- Does a strategic plan exist?
- Are the goals and objectives clear and measurable, is an individual accountable for them, and is there a timeline for their completion?
- Are the goals and objectives known and understood by the school community?
- Is the planning process ongoing?

THE CHANGE PROCESS

Perhaps the most important element in an organization's development is how it responds and adapts to change. In order to bring about effective change, the leader must draw together his or her knowledge and skills in all the other components of organizational development. The process of change is so important to the organizational development of an institution that I devote an entire chapter to the process.

NOTES

1. Robert H. Palestini, *The Ten-Minute Guide to Educational Leadership* (Lancaster: Technomic Publishing, 1998).

2. Peter Senge, "The Leader's New Work: Building Learning Organizations," *Sloan Management Review* (Fall 1990): 7–23.

3. William Glasser, *Control Theory* (New York: Harper & Row, 1985).

4. Abraham H. Maslow, *Motivation and Personality*, 3rd ed. (New York: Harper & Row, 1987).

5. E. L. Thorndike, *Behaviorism* (New York: Norton, 1924).

6. B. A. Mellers, "Equity Judgment, a Revision of Aristotelian Views," *Journal of Experimental Psychology* 111 (1982): 42–270.

7. R. Vance and A. Colella, "Effects of Two Types of Feedback on Goal Acceptance and Personal Goals," *Journal of Applied Psychology* 75 (1990): 68–76.

8. R. E. Zuker, *Mastering Assertativeness Skills* (New York: AMACOM, 1983).

9. A. J. Lange and P. Jokubowski, *Responsible Assertive Behavior* (Champaign, IL: Research Press, 1976).

10. Robert H. Palestini, *Educational Administration: Leading with Mind and Heart* (Lancaster: Technomic Publishing, 1999).

11. Wayne Hoy and Cecil Miskel, *Educational Administration*, 5th ed. (New York: McGraw-Hill, 1996).

12. V. H. Vroom and P. W. Yetton, *Leadership and Decision Making* (Pittsburgh: University of Pittsburgh Press, 1973).

13. L. K. Trevino, "Ethical Decision Making in Organizations: A Person Situation Interactionist Model," *Academy of Management Review* 11 (1986): 601–617.

14. J. S. Carroll and E. J. Johnson, *Decision Research: A Field Guide* (Newbury Park, CA: Sage, 1990).

15. P. C. Nutt, "Types of Organizational Decision Process," *Administrative Science Quarterly* 29 (1984): 414–450.

16. J. P. Kolter, "Why Power and Influence Issues Are at the Very Core of Executive Work," in *Executive Power*, ed. S. Srivastva et al. (San Francisco: Jossey-Bass, 1986).

17. Henry Mintzberg, *Power In and Around Organizations* (Englewood Cliffs, NJ: Prentice Hall, 1983).

18. R. M. Emerson, "Power-Dependence Relations," *American Sociological Review* 27 (1962): 31–41.

19. R. Fisher and W. Ury, *Getting to Yes: Negotiating Without Giving In* (Boston: Houghton Mifflin, 1981).

CHAPTER 7

Implications for Institutional Change

In an earlier work entitled *The Ten-Minute Guide to Educational Leadership*, I suggest that if educational leaders systematically focus on ten aspects of their institution each day, they will most likely be effective. These ten components include the school's organizational structure, its organizational climate, its leadership, motivation, communication, planning, decision making, and conflict-management processes, its power distribution, and its attitude toward change. Of these essential elements, I believe that an institution's tolerance of and ability to change is the most important element for success. I also believe that mastering the ability to effect change successfully to transform an institution is the culminating activity of the effective educational leader.

Successfully effecting change requires the educational leader to have mastered all of the other elements necessary for promoting organizational effectiveness. To effect successful change, the educational administrator must have outstanding leadership skills, ensure that the organizational structure is appropriate, engender a climate of trust and respect, motivate his or her colleagues to achieve a vision, communicate effectively, plan strategically, incorporate appropriate decision-making techniques, effectively manage conflict, and empower faculty and staff. This is a daunting task—so daunting that the average educational administrator is not able to cope with it. As a result, successful implementation of change in the form of educational reform remains the exception rather than the rule, as do effective educational institutions. The question now is, how do we incorporate the philosophy of administration espoused here into the effective implementation of the change process?

MAKING CHANGE HAPPEN

Education, particularly urban public education, seems to be in a continual state of crisis. None of its constituencies seems to be satisfied with its outcomes. There is no dearth of remedies, however. Educational research has produced a variety of reforms that the scholars claim will resolve many of the problems encountered in American education. Until now, however, the major problem has been how to implement these reforms effectively. There have been sporadic successes, but generalizing from these effective models has been problematic.

Reforms, such as site-based management, charter schools, clustering, whole-language instruction, cooperative learning, outcomes-based education, distance education, and the constructivist classroom all have their advocates. Pilot programs using these approaches and others have been successful. The frustration lies in how to implement these reforms universally so that the schools where they are effective become the rule rather than the exception. In a nutshell, the issue becomes, how do we successfully effect change? Basically, looking at an institution in the terms described above is in the functionalist-structuralist tradition. The remaining question is, how do we imbue this approach with the principles of critical theory and the Ignatian vision?

Emotionally, we seem to prefer the status quo. Intellectually, however, we all seem to realize that to progress, we need to experience change. Collectively, we have bought into Edwards Deming's notion that for any institution to thrive, "continuous improvement" is an absolute necessity. Earlier in this text, we have seen that the *magis* principle also implies change. But none of this rationalizing makes it any easier to accept change as a way of life. When dealing with the process of change, we seem to operate on a visceral level. Our security needs seem to clash with our achievement needs, and our security needs frequently prevail. Nevertheless, if our educational institutions are to progress, we need to overcome our instincts and implement the reforms that will make them effective in educating our children and adults.

AN INTEGRATED APPROACH TO CHANGE

The literature is replete with various suggested change processes, more or less based on functionalist-structuralist theory. Many of them contain elements that are helpful in leading to a successful transformation, but few contain all of the necessary components. As a result, through the process of trial and error, I have developed my own process for change. I call it an integrated change process because although there are distinct steps in the process, the key to their successful implementation is that many of them are implemented simultaneously rather than sequentially.

In an earlier work, entitled *Ten Steps to Educational Reform: Making Change Happen*, we suggest the following steps in the process:

1. Establishing a climate for change
2. Assessing the need for change
3. Creating a sense of urgency
4. Assessing favorable and opposing forces
5. Selecting among alternatives
6. Promoting ownership
7. Providing professional development
8. Operationalizing the change
9. Evaluating the change
10. Institutionalizing the change

Most attempts at effecting change in the form of educational reform fail because leaders have no plan at all or do not engage in all the steps in the process. Other failures occur when administrators try to implement the reform by following the change process steps sequentially rather than simultaneously and get bogged down in one or another of the steps, unable to bring the process to closure.

Whether it be an apparently insignificant change, such as deciding between the homogenous or the heterogeneous grouping of students (tracking) or what form of assessment should be used in college admission, or a more significant reform, such as whether tuition vouchers should be used to restructure and reform public education, we are suggesting that the implementation of these steps be viewed through the lens of critical theory and the Ignatian vision. Let us now see how functionalism, critical theory and the Ignatian vision impacts each of the steps in the integrated change process.

ESTABLISHING A CLIMATE FOR CHANGE

E. Mark Hanson, in his text entitled *Educational Administration and Organizational Behavior*, describes an incident regarding the process of change. Always interested in the processes of school improvement, he once asked the superintendent of a large, urban school district, "How does change come about around here?" She thought for a moment. "Well," she replied, "there is the normal way and the miraculous way. The normal way," she continued, "is where the heavens part and the angels come down and do the change for us. The miraculous way is when we do it ourselves."[1]

If you have established a climate of change at your institution, change will come to be expected. It will be perceived as something positive and routine. The need for change in the context of continuous improvement should be articulated constantly by institutional leaders. College presidents, superintendents, and principals should set the tone for change by taking every opportunity to articulate its necessity and model it in their own leadership. For example, the faculty convocations can be occasions for articulating the notion that if the institution is to progress, academically and operationally, it must be open to change. At the initial meeting, the possible changes that are anticipated during the upcoming academic year can be shared. At subsequent faculty meetings, the need for change can be reinforced. Using the establishment of a climate for change as the first step in a systematic method of effecting change is a functionalist-structuralist principle. Articulating the need for change, modeling change, and establishing trust and respect are behaviors that are the product of utilizing critical theory and the Ignatian vision, specifically the *magis* principle and secular humanism.

In addition to articulating the need for change, to promote a positive school climate the leader must model a tolerance for change. Even if it is something simple, such as changing the color of the school lockers every two or three years or changing the format of faculty meetings to incorporate innovative concepts like cooperative learning and shared decision making, the leader needs to lead by example. The leader must be perceived as being open to new ideas and providing a climate in which creativity is fostered. In other words, "be the change that you expect in others."

While fostering a climate for change, the leader must be careful not to be perceived as being in favor of change for its own sake, or for his or her own sake. If this occurs, it can have a counterproductive or dysfunctional effect. One way of precluding such a perception is to mutually establish the basics or essentials of your institution—the things that are relatively constant and not subject to change—and those that must change for your institution to remain healthy. Such fundamentals as academic excellence, individual attention, community involvement, and an emphasis on educational outcomes might be identified as remaining constant, while instructional methods, curricular approaches, and organizational structure are subject to change. In other words, the goals can remain constant for awhile, while the methods of achieving them may be frequently changing. In establishing both the goals and the methods, however, remember to examine them under the lens of critical theory by being aware of the equitable distribution of power, and so forth, and the Ignatian vision, by being aware of the social justice implications, and so forth.

Another way to avoid being perceived as in favor of change for change's sake is to be certain that when a change is implemented, all of the steps in the process are followed. If this is done, first, it is more likely that the change will be implemented successfully, and second, if the change is not effective, the evaluation stage of the process provides an opportunity to move away from it gracefully. In addition, success breeds success. If the leader has a record of implementing change successfully, it paves the way for future change. If leaders also have a reputation for objectively evaluating the effectiveness of change and abandoning it if it is unsuccessful, they will foster a climate with a high tolerance for change.

If a positive climate for change is to be established, another requisite is an environment of trust and respect. Institutions do not amount to anything without the people who make them what they are. The individuals most influential in making institutions what they are, are essentially volunteers. Our very best teachers and administrators can work anywhere they please. So, in a sense, they volunteer to work where they do. As educational leaders, we would do far better if we looked on and treated our employees as volunteers. To engender trust and respect in the Ignatian tradition, we should treat our employees as if we had a covenantal, rather than contractual, relationship with them. We will speak more on covenantal relationships in the next chapter.

If an educational institution is to be a place where change is not only tolerated, but embraced, it must be successful in creating a culture of trust and respect so that everyone in it feels as if he or she "owns the place." We often hear educators refer to where they work as "school," such as "I will be staying at school late tonight, dear." On the other hand, beware of the teacher who says simply, "I will be staying at work late tonight." That teacher has likely not taken "ownership" in the place.

Taking ownership is a sign of one's love for an institution. In his book, *Servant Leadership*, Robert Greenleaf says, "Love is an undefinable term, and its manifestations are both subtle and infinite. It has only one absolute condition: unlimited liability!"[2] Although it may run counter to our traditional notion of American capitalism, employees should be encouraged to act as if they "own the place"; it is a sign of love, and it is a prerequisite for establishing a positive climate for change.

Diagnostic Checklist

Here are a few questions that you can address in assessing your institution's climate for change:

- Is the need for change being articulated constantly?
- Is the institution's leadership modeling change?
- Is a climate of trust and respect being nurtured?
- Are the leaders engaging in effective change behavior?

ASSESSING A NEED

The next step in the integrated change process is the needs assessment. Unfortunately, this step is often ignored. Many educational leaders become enamored of one educational reform or another and try to implement it whether or not there is an identified and agreed upon need. Reforms, such as the whole-language approach to reading, cooperative learning, block scheduling, interdisciplinary curricula, distance learning, and even site-based management, have been adopted arbitrarily by misguided educational administrators. When implemented without a needs assessment, or at least an after-the-fact needs assessment, these changes are destined to fail. Both critical theory and the Ignatian vision call on us to be inclusive and empowering in the process of establishing a need. Faculty and staff input is essential for success.

Ordinarily a needs assessment calls for a review of existing data and may require some surveying of clients and other appropriate reference groups. There is always a certain risk in a needs assessment. In the process of uncovering needs, one may also raise expectations that all of the respondent's concerns will be addressed. Fundamental to effecting change is priority setting and focus; thus, not all needs can be met immediately. Resources are in short supply, and difficult, sometimes painful decisions have to be made about which from an array of critical needs requires attention. Three reference groups are especially important to the needs assessment and the change process: students and parents, professional staff, and educational policy makers. Oftentimes, it is the students or parents who are left out of the process. Leaving them out, of course, has distribution-of-power implications and is a violation of the principles of critical theory and the Ignatian vision.

Data about students are readily available in the records a typical school generates and maintains. Standardized test scores, attendance records, free- or reduced-price-lunch recipients, analyses of students with disabilities, transportation reports, and a host of other official and unofficial sources provide basic data when it comes time to develop a profile of the students in the school or school district. Informal discussions with colleagues, other professionals, and the students and parents themselves are another source of information. Student focus groups and systematic observation by both teachers and administrators are still other ways of assessing whether there is a need for change in the school.

Use of community and parent surveys can be very helpful to the school leader, as can community advisory groups. Such surveys are invaluable in determining parent and community expectations and attitudes and perceptions of the educational needs of the community's young people. The diverse nature of most communities requires that in any survey care be taken that the necessary degree of randomness exists. Concern for complete information and diversity of opinion should also be reflected in the composition of advisory groups.

Another source of information regarding the needs of the school is the professional staff. They can be helpful with regard to instructional and curricular needs and can offer specific observations about the nature of the student body. Staff surveys or any of a number of rational problem-solving processes are useful in needs assessments. Using some of these methods in combination can be effective. For example, a faculty meeting may be used to brainstorm the strengths and weaknesses of the institution. The information could then be summarized and items generated for a survey to determine the perceived intensity and importance of the issues identified. The nominal group technique or the Delphi technique can then be used.

Central office personnel, local and state board members, state department of education, legislators, the federal Department of Education, education advocacy groups, accrediting groups, and other such entities are examples of educational policy makers. They also should be consulted to identify the needs of the educational institution. Lastly, the reports of accrediting associations, such as the Middle States Association, Phi Beta Kappa, and the American Association of Colleges and Schools of Business (AACSB), can be valuable tools for assessing the needs of an institution.

Diagnostic Checklist

Here are a few questions you can address in assessing whether your institution has identified a need for change:

- Have data been collected that indicate a need for change in your institution?
- Has a formal or informal needs assessment taken place?
- Did the needs assessment survey reflect the mission and beliefs of the institution?
- Has the needs assessment corroborated the anecdotal data?
- Has the need for the identified change been promulgated to the school community?

CREATING A SENSE OF URGENCY

Because our natural instinct is to resist change, to effect a needed change, a sense of alarm or urgency must often be created. To overcome our innate sense of inertia, the dire consequences of remaining in the status quo need to be articulated. There are a number of ways to create a sense of urgency, including citing comparable data and projected enrollment declines. But in creating a sense of urgency, the change agent must be aware that individuals and groups are often moved by dissimilar forces. In other words, what may cause a sense of urgency in one person may not do so in another.

Creating a sense of urgency or stress can have both functional and dysfunctional outcomes. Whether stress takes a constructive or destructive course is influenced by the sociocultural context in which the stress occurs because differences tend to exaggerate barriers and reduce the likelihood of conflict resolution. The issues involved also will affect the likely outcomes. Whether the individuals or groups have cooperative, individualistic, or competitive orientations toward stress will affect the outcomes as well.

Effective educational administrators learn how to create functional conflict and manage dysfunctional conflict. They develop and practice techniques for diagnosing the causes and nature of stress and transform it into a productive force that fosters needed change in the institution. Many universities, for example, have healthy competition among their schools (e.g., Business College, College of Arts and Sciences, College of Education) for recruitment of the most qualified students. This is an example of a functional sense of urgency or stress.

One can see, then, that some stress is beneficial. It can encourage organizational innovation, creativity, and adaptation. For example, a number of nonpublic-school systems, and even some public ones, allow schools within the system to compete for the same students. This open-enrollment, or "public-school choice," policy often spawns innovation and change in marketing techniques and, more important, in curriculum and instruction. In these cases, creating a sense of urgency can result in more employee enthusiasm and better decision making. The challenge is to be able to create a sense of urgency without allowing it to become dysfunctional. This means that the change agent must know the stages of stress and when to intervene. In addition, if we adhere to the Ignatian concept of *cura personalis*, we have an obligation to avoid creating dysfunctional stress in our colleagues.

Diagnostic Checklist

Here are a few questions you can address in assessing whether a sense of urgency has been created:

- Has the school community been taken to the perceived stress stage of development?
- Have compelling arguments been developed for the change?
- Have they been applied to the appropriate constituencies?
- Has a position paper on the change been developed and distributed?

ASSESSING FAVORABLE AND OPPOSING FORCES

Accurate assessment of the forces that affect proposed reform is possibly the most important step in the integrated change process. Correctly identifying the forces that favor the reform and those that oppose it is crucial to effective implementation of the change. Further, the interventions chosen to neutralize the forces against change and enhance the forces in favor of it are instrumental to its eventual success.

The forces resistant to change can be considerable. These forces range from the simple ignorance of an individual to the complex vested interests of our own institutions' members. As the comic strip character Pogo phrased it, "We have met the enemy and he is us."

The forces resistant to change are an important part of the organization's environment or climate. They must be diagnosed, understood, and taken into account in the targeting process and in selecting a change strategy. The environment harboring the forces of resistance is typically not social or technical, but sociotechnical. A sociotechnical interpretation of environment refers to the behavior of individuals as it is shaped by the interaction of technical characteristics, such as instructional equipment, physical layout of the school, activity schedules, and social characteristics, such as norms, informal groups, power centers, and the like. As Chin and Benne point out, "The problem-solving structures and processes of a human system must be developed to deal with a range of sociotechnical difficulties, converting them into problems and organizing the relevant processes of data collection, planning, invention, and tryout of solutions, evaluation and feedback of results, replanning, and so forth, which are required for the solution of the problem."[3]

According to Richard Carlson, a major organizational feature that contributes to resistance to change is the domestication of public schools and other educational institutions. A domesticated organization has many properties of the monopoly: It does not have to compete for resources, except in a very limited area; it has a steady flow of clients; and its survival is guaranteed.[4] Although private schools and colleges do not possess all of these characteristics in the way that public schools do, many of the teachers view their institutions in this way. One often hears the college professor or the private-school teacher proclaim in the light of declining enrollments, "That's the administration's problem."

Because these institutions are domesticated organizations, they do not face the problems of private organizations that make it necessary to build major change mechanisms into their structures. Change capability permits private organizations to make the necessary modifications in production and product continually to hold their share of the market and expand it if possible. The domestication of the school builds in a layer of protective insulation that cannot be penetrated easily. Thus, to effect change in a domesticated organization becomes a greater challenge.

An interesting example of this type of organizational behavior was part of California's omnibus educational reform bill of 1983, which was intended to increase instructional time in the classroom. A comparative study had shown that California's students received 2.5 weeks less instructional time than the national average. The bill offered financial incentives to districts to meet the target of 180 days a year and 240 minutes a day at a cost of $250 million annually for the first three years. The average high school needed to add four days to its school year and six minutes each day to qualify for the incentive award of $75 per pupil. The average elementary school needed to add four days for a $55-per-pupil-per-day bonus.

In light of a potential contract violation and teachers' resistance to increased instructional time without increased compensation, districts found creative ways to lengthen the school day and year without increasing instructional time. Some districts added one minute to each passing period between classes, which could add up to 900 minutes or about eighteen 50-minute classes. Other schools extended homeroom periods by 5 minutes each day, totaling 900 minutes per year. Others added an extra recess to the school day. Some schools did add one or two minutes of instructional time to each class. When considering educational change in a domesticated organization, therefore, the result is not always the desired outcome.

Goodwin Watson points out that during the process of effecting change, perceived resistance moves through a four-stage cycle. He describes the arrival of a reform in these terms: "In the early stage, when only a few pioneer thinkers take the reform seriously, resistance appears massive and undifferentiated. 'Everyone' knows better; 'No one in his right mind' could advocate the change. Proponents are labeled crack-pots or visionaries."

In the second stage some support becomes evident, the pro and con forces become visible, and the lines of battle are drawn. In the third stage the battle is engaged "as resistance becomes mobilized to crush the upstart proposal." The supporters of the change are often surprised and frequently overwhelmed by the opposition's tenacity. Survival of the innovation depends on developing a base of power to overcome the opposition.

If the supporters of change are victorious in the third stage, the fourth stage is characterized by support flowing to the newly arrived reform. "The persisting resistance is, at this stage, seen as a stubborn, hidebound, cantankerous nuisance. For a time, the danger of a counter-swing of the pendulum remains real." The cycle begins anew when another effort toward change occurs.[5]

FORCE-FIELD ANALYSIS

To understand the forces that affect a change, we can use an analytical technique called force-field analysis, which views a problem as a product of forces working in different, often opposite directions. An organization, or any of its subsystems, maintains the status quo when the sum of opposing forces is zero. When forces in one direction exceed forces in the opposite one, the organization or subsystem moves in the direction of the greater forces. For example, if forces for change exceed forces against change, then change is likely to occur.

To move the educational institution toward a different desired state requires increasing the forces for change in that direction, decreasing the forces against change in that direction, or both. Generally, reducing resistance forces creates less tension in the system and fewer unanticipated consequences than increasing forces for change. Suppose your institution was moving from homogenous to heterogeneous grouping. Reducing the resistance to the changes created by the introduction of heterogeneous grouping increases the likelihood of the changeover. When the administrators and staff no longer resist change, the present state moves closer to the desired state.

Consider again our example of heterogeneous grouping. Moving from homogenous grouping in the form of tracking to the more egalitarian heterogeneous grouping is bound to encounter resistance. What are the opposing forces that one can anticipate? Certainly some of the teaching staff will be against the change because it will entail more small-group instruction and adapting their lesson plans to a variety of ability levels. On the contrary, what are the forces in favor of change? Once again, one can anticipate that certain of the faculty, especially the critical pedagogues, will favor the more egalitarian approach that is embodied in heterogeneous grouping. A savvy administrator will be able to apply interventions that would neutralize the opposition and mobilize the forces in favor of this change. Using force-field analysis in a systematic way can be very helpful in bringing about desired change.

Changes in the organization's environment, such as new laws or regulations, rapidly increasing competition, or an unpredictable rate of inflation, may require the organization to implement new structures or reward systems. New programs resulting from the availability of improved technology; changes in competition in education; or unusual requirements of the new generation of students, such as inclusion or mainstreaming, may also affect the institution.

Finally, reduced productivity and effectiveness, product quality, satisfaction, commitment, or increased turnover or absenteeism may call for changes in intra- or international relations. One or two specific events external to the institution frequently precipitate the change. For example, the publication of *A Nation at Risk* in the 1980s caused a flurry of educational reforms that continue to this day. The events at Columbine High School are another example of how an external event can effect change in your own institution.

Forces known as resistance forces counteract the forces for change. Administrators might resist changes to their routines and supervisory activities; they may also be unwilling to relinquish their decision-making authority. Superintendents may be unwilling to allocate the resources required to change the culture. Identifying and then reducing resistance forces may be essential to making an individual or group receptive to change.

Forces against a change often reside within the institution and stem from rigid organizational structures and individual thinking. Specific forces against change include employees' distrust of the change agent, fear of change, desire to maintain power, and complacency; lack of resources to support the change; conflicts between individual and organizational goals; and organizational inertia against changing the status quo. These forces frequently combine into significant resistance to change.

Resistance results from a variety of factors. First, it occurs when a change ignores the needs, attitudes, and beliefs of an organization's members. If teachers, for example, have high security needs, they may see as threatening the increased attention to distance learning. Second, individuals resist change when they lack specific information about the change; they may not know when, how, or why it is occurring. Third, individuals may not perceive a need for change; they may feel that their organization is operating effectively and efficiently. In these cases change often is neither voluntary nor requested by organization members. Fourth, organization members frequently have a we-they mentality that causes them to view the change agent as their enemy, particularly when change is imposed by representatives outside of the immediate work site. Fifth, members may view change as a threat to the prestige and security of the institution. They may perceive the change in procedures or policies as a commentary that their performance is inadequate. Sixth, employees may perceive the change as a threat to their expertise, status, or security. Introduction of a new computer-aided instructional system, for example, may cause teachers to feel that they lack sufficient knowledge to perform their jobs; revision of an organization's structure may challenge their relative status in the organization; introduction of a new reward system may threaten their feelings of job security. For effective change to occur, the change agent must confront each of these factors and overcome the resulting resistance. It helps a great deal if the change agent has engendered a sense of mutual trust and respect among his or her colleagues before the effort to effect change begins.

The implications of structural functionalism, critical theory, and the Ignatian tradition on dealing with the resistance to change are many. The use of force-field analysis recommended here to facilitate the change process implies a structural-functionalist view of the educational administration. We are assuming that by using this model, we will have a better chance of effecting successful change. This implies that there is a systematic, rational method of arriving at a positive result, even when dealing with the unpredictability of human nature.

As we discussed earlier, many administrators might deal with opposing forces with equal force. Human nature provokes many of us "to fight fire with fire." As critical pedagogues and Ignatian humanists, however, we concern ourselves with sharing power and influence, not with eliminating it. Thus, in the process of applying force-field analysis, we must be careful to use compelling argument rather than coercion to neutralize opposing forces. Likewise, when we are developing and selecting alternatives, we must be careful to make the process inclusionary rather than exclusionary. Participative decision making needs to be employed, and group decision making should be the rule rather than the exception. We will discuss this in greater detail in the next section.

The principles prescribed by the critical theory and the Ignatian tradition would require that in the process of addressing the resistant forces to change, we be careful to inspire our colleagues, but not manipulate them. Not only do our overall goals have to be laudable, but so do the means by which we reach them. So, in utilizing the structural-functionalist strategies suggested here, we must continually be concerned with the equitable distribution of power, the need to be other-centered rather than self-centered, the prevention of the mindless perpetuation of the dominant culture, the care of the person, and solidarity with the underserved. If we view our leadership behavior through these lenses, I argue that a culture of mutual trust and respect will be developed and needed change will be more readily accepted.

Diagnostic Checklist

Here are a few questions you can address about your institution's assessment of forces:

- Is a force-field analysis being performed?
- Is it adequately identifying favorable and opposing forces?
- Is there a systematic plan to affirm and strengthen the favorable forces?
- Is there a systematic plan to neutralize the opposing forces?

DEVELOPING AND SELECTING ALTERNATIVES

While the above-mentioned steps in the integrated change process are being addressed, the change agent should establish a committee or task force of "believers" to begin developing alternatives that would address the perceived need for change. Ideally, a deliberative consideration of the various alternatives should be undertaken, and the most cost-efficient and effective alternative should be chosen. All too often, however, "the powers that be" have chosen the alternative already and the change agent is expected simply to implement it. Of course, "the powers that be" in this instance would certainly not have been utilizing the principles espoused here if they determined the change by fiat. In these instances, however, the change agent should at the very least be free to adapt the reform to meet local needs.

Another phenomenon that sometimes occurs during this phase of the change process is the tendency to satisfice, or choose the alternative that offends the fewest individuals or groups, rather than choosing the best alternative. Satisficing is a term coined by Herbert Simon, a Nobel Prize winner in economics, who was critical of the so-called rational model of decision making, which indicates that decision makers develop and analyze all of the possible alternatives and select the best one available. Dr. Simon was apparently an early devotee of critical theory.[6]

According to Simon, at a certain point in the decision-making process, rather than choosing the best possible alternative, in the interest of efficiency the decision maker will satisfice, or sacrifice the optimal for a solution or alternative that is satisfactory or good enough. For example, if a school is trying to decide between the traditional phonics approach versus the whole-language approach to teaching reading, the change agent(s) may satisfice and choose an integrated model that combines the best aspects of both the phonics and whole-language approaches. Thus, the change agent may sacrifice the optimal solution for one that satisfies the greatest number of constituencies.

In a similar approach to selecting an alternative, the model known as decision making by objection prompts decision makers not to seek an optimal solution to a problem, but to choose a course of action that does not have a high probability of making matters worse. The decision makers first produce a rough description of an acceptable resolution of the situation. Then they propose a course of action, accompanied by a description of the positive outcomes of the action. Objections to the action are raised, further delimiting the problem and defining an acceptable resolution. The decision makers repeat this process, crating a series of courses of action, each one raising fewer objections than the previous one. Finally, the most acceptable alternative evolves. On the surface, this approach seems to violate the *magis* principle, but Ignatius tells us that where the greatest good is not attainable, the greater good is sometimes acceptable.

Once the force-field analysis described earlier has been completed, it is time to generate alternatives that could be implemented to address the identified need effectively. Generally a small committee representing as many of the institution's constituencies as appropriate should be established. The members of the committee should be those who are advocates of change with possibly a naysayer or two included as "devil's advocates." In preparation for their work, committee members should be provided with the latest research findings regarding the reform being considered and be encouraged to make themselves aware of successful uses of the alternatives being considered. The so-called best-practices approach can be effective in identifying possible alternatives and convincing staff members of the reform's efficacy. The alternative that is finally chosen should be the one that best fits the local needs and should be selected according to its (1) rationale, (2) proven effectiveness, (3) resource requirements, (4) distinctive qualities, (5) mission appropriateness, and (6) cost-benefit ratio.

The next logical question that the structural functionalist might ask is how can change agents overcome barriers, reduce biases, and make more effective decisions regarding the selection of the appropriate re-form alternative? There are at least three techniques that can improve the alternative development and selection process: (1) brainstorming, (2) the nominal group technique, and (3) the Delphi technique.

Groups of individuals use brainstorming to generate many alternatives for consideration in the selection process. In brainstorming, the group lists as many alternatives as possible without evaluating the feasibility of any alternative. For example, if a cost-reduction program is needed in a school district to offset continuing budget deficits, the change agent might be charged with listing all of the ways of reducing costs in a school system. The absence of evaluation encourages group members to generate rather than defend ideas. Then, after ideas have been generated, they are evaluated, and selections are made. Although brainstorming can result in many shallow and useless ideas, it can also motivate members to offer new and innovative ideas. It works best when individuals have a common view of what constitutes a good idea, but it is more difficult to use when specialized knowledge or complex implementation is required. Because most educational reforms are complex in nature, brainstorming can only be used effectively in a limited number of cases and as part of the alternative-generation process rather than the alternative-selection process.

The nominal group technique is a structured group meeting that helps resolve differences in group opinion by having individuals generate and then rank-order a series of ideas in the problem-solving, alternative-generation, or decision-making stage of a planning process. A group of individuals is presented with a stated problem. Each person individually offers alternative solutions in writing. The group then shares the solutions and lists them on a chart, as in brainstorming. Group members discuss and clarify the ideas, then they rank and vote their preference for the various ideas. If the group has not reached an agreement, they repeat the ranking and voting procedure until the group reaches some agreement.

The size of the group and the diverse expertise of its members increase the usefulness of the nominal group technique. It encourages each group member to think individually and offer ideas about the content of a proposal, and then directs group discussion. It moves the group toward problem resolution by systematically focusing on top-ranked ideas and eliminating less-valued ones. The nominal group technique also encourages continued exploration of the issues, provides a forum for the expression of minority viewpoints, gives individuals some time to think about the issues before offering solutions, and provides a mechanism for reaching a decision expediently through the ranking-voting procedure. It fosters creativity by allowing extensive individual input into the process. Strong personality types dominate the group less often because of the opportunity for systematic input by all group members. It encourages innovation, limits conflict, emphasizes equal participation by all members, helps generate consensus, and incorporates the preferences of individuals in decision-making choices. However, unless the change agent is trained in the use of this technique, it is more prudent to use an organizational consultant trained in these techniques to act as a facilitator.

The Delphi technique structures group communication by dealing with a complex problem in four phases: (1) exploration of the subject by individuals, (2) reaching an understanding of the group's view of the issues, (3) sharing and evaluating any reasons for differences, and (4) final evaluation of all information. In the conventional Delphi, a small group designs a questionnaire, which is completed by a larger respondent group; the results are then tabulated and used in developing a revised questionnaire, which is again completed by the larger group. Thus, the results of the original polling are fed back to the respondent group to use in subsequent responses. This procedure is repeated until the issues are narrowed, responses are focused, or consensus is reached. In another format, a computer summarizes the results, thus replacing the small group. Such group-decision support systems have increased the focus on the task or problem, the depth of analysis, communication about the task and clarifying information and conclusions, effort expended by the group, widespread participation of group members, and consensus reaching.

Delphi is very helpful in a variety of circumstances. First, if the decision makers cannot apply precise analytical techniques to solving the problem, but prefer to use subjective judgments on a collective basis, Delphi can provide input from a large number of respondents. Second, if the individuals involved have failed to communicate effectively in the past, the Delphi procedures offer a systematic method for ensuring that their opinions are presented. Third, the Delphi does not require face-to-face interaction, so it succeeds when the group is too large for such a direct exchange. Fourth, when time and cost prevent frequent group meetings or when additional premeeting communication between group members increases the efficiency of the meeting held, the Delphi technique offers significant value for decision making. Fifth, the Delphi can overcome situations where individuals disagree strongly or where anonymity of views must be maintained to protect group members. Finally, the Delphi technique reduces the likelihood of groupthink; it prevents one or more members from dominating by their numbers or strength of personality.

On another issue related to developing alternatives, we often hear about the alleged virtue of bottom-up versus top-down strategies for generating educational reforms. In fact, utilizing the principles of critical theory and the Ignatian vision would prompt us to prefer the bottom-up approach. Thus, it is the minority view that top-down strategies are more effective. The fact of the matter is that neither of these strategies is maximally effective in isolation. Rather, coordinating top-down and bottom-up strategies for educational reform is most effective.

Small- and large-scale studies of top-down strategies have demonstrated consistently that local implementation fails in the vast majority of cases. The best known study of voluntary adoption of top-down movements is the Rand Change Agent study conducted by Berman and McLaughlin and associates. They investigated federally sponsored educational programs adopted in 293 sites and found that, even though adoption was voluntary, districts often took on change projects for opportunistic rather than substantial reasons.[7]

On a more sweeping scale, Sarason argues that billions of dollars have been spent on top-down reforms with little to show for it. Sarason observes that such reform efforts do have an implicit theory of change: Change can come about by proclaiming new policies, or by legislation, or by setting new performance standards, or by creating a shape-up-or-ship-out ambiance, or by all of the preceding. It is a conception that in principle is similar to how you go about creating and improving an assembly line—that is, what it means to those who work on the assembly line is of secondary significance, if it has any significance at all. The workers will change.[8]

In short, centralized reform mandates have a poor track record as instruments for educational improvement. This failure has led some to conclude that only decentralized, locally driven reform can succeed. Site-based management, or giving more decision-making power to the local level, is currently the most prominent manifestation of this focus. So far, however, the claim to superiority of grassroots initiatives is primarily theoretical. In reviewing evidence on site-based management in *The New Meaning of Educational Change*, one can conclude that restructuring reforms that involved decision making by schools may have altered governance procedures, but they do not affect the teaching-learning process in any significant way.[9]

The evidence that bottom-up strategies are no more effective than top-down ones continues to mount. Taylor and Teddlie draw similar conclusions in their study of the extent of classroom change in "a district widely acclaimed as a model of restructuring." They examined classrooms in 33 schools (16 from pilot schools that had established site-based management programs and 17 from nonpilot schools in the same district). They did find that teachers in the pilot schools reported higher levels of participation in decision making, but they found no differences in teaching strategies (teacher-directed instruction and low student involvement dominated in both sets of cases). Further, there was little evidence of teacher-teacher collaboration. Extensive collaboration was reported in only 2 of the 33 schools, and both were nonpilot schools. Taylor and Teddlie observe, "Teachers in this study did not alter their practice. . . . Increasing their participation in decision making did not overcome norms of autonomy so that teachers would feel empowered to collaborate with their colleagues."[10] In sum, then, decentralized initiatives do not fare any better than centralized reforms.

A number of educational researchers have concluded that organizations, including schools, that underwent successful revitalization followed a particular sequence in which individual, small-group, and informal behavior began to change first (bottom-up, if you will), which in turn was reinforced and further propelled by changes in formal design and procedures (structures, personnel practices, compensation systems, etc.) in the organization (top-down). Both local and central levels can be active and influential at all phases. These studies and my own experience have led me to promote an integrated change process that involves both top-down and bottom-up strategies that operate simultaneously in effectively implemented reform.

Top-down strategies result in conflict, or superficial compliance, or both. Expecting local units to flourish through laissez-fare decentralization leads to drift, narrowness, or inertia. Combined strategies that capitalize on the central office' strengths (to provide direction, incentives, networking, and monitoring) and the local institution's capacities (to learn, create, respond, and contribute) are more likely to achieve greater overall effectiveness. Such systems also have greater accountability, given that the need to obtain political support for ideas is built into their pattern of interaction.

Simultaneous top-down/bottom-up strategies are essential because dynamically complex societies are full of surprises. Only the negotiated capacity and strengths of the entire school community are capable of promoting school improvement while retaining the capacity to learn from new patterns, whether anticipated or not. Finally, one level cannot wait for the other level to act. Systems do not change by themselves; individuals and groups change systems. Breakthroughs occur when productive connections amass, creating growing pressure for systems to change. The more that top-down and bottom-up forces are coordinated, the more likely complex systems are to move toward greater effectiveness.

Diagnostic Checklist

Here are a few questions you can address in assessing your institution's success in creating and selecting alternatives:

- Is creative thinking being used in developing possible alternatives?
- Are representatives of all segments of the school community involved in the selection process?
- Does the alternative selected relate to local needs?
- Are both top-down and bottom-up strategies being employed?

PROMOTING A SENSE OF OWNERSHIP

It is a truism in education, and in other fields as well, that if a change or reform is to be implemented successfully, it must have the support of the faculty and staff. Consequently, we often hear managers suggest that a new program does not have a chance of succeeding unless the employees take ownership of it. Most of us agree with the common sense of this assertion. But how does a leader effectively promote employee ownership? Let us suggest four steps that embody critical theory and the Ignatian vision as a beginning:

1. Respect people. As we have indicated earlier, this starts with appreciating the diverse gifts that individuals bring to your organization. The key is to dwell on the strengths of your coworkers, rather than on their weaknesses. This does not mean that disciplinary action, or even dismissal, will never become necessary. It does mean, however, that we should focus on the formative aspect of the employee-evaluation process before we engage in the summative part. Leaders are obligated to develop colleagues' skills and place them in situations that will maximize their potential for success.

2. Let belief guide policy and practice. We spoke earlier of developing a culture of civility in an institution. If there is an environment of mutual respect and trust, the institution will flourish. Leaders need to let their belief or value systems guide their behavior. Style is merely a consequence of what we believe and what is in our hearts.

3. Recognize the need for covenants. Contractual agreements cover such things as salary, fringe benefits, and working conditions. They are part of organizational life, and there is a legitimate need for them. But in today's educational institutions, where the best people working in our schools are similar to volunteers, we need covenantal relationships. Our best workers may choose their employers. They usually choose the institution where they work based on reasons less tangible than salaries and fringe benefits. They do not need contracts; they need covenants. Covenantal relationships enable educational institutions to be civil, hospitable, and understanding of individuals' differences and unique natures. They allow administrators to recognize that treating everyone equally is not necessarily treating everyone fairly. Sometimes exceptions need to be made, and certain individuals need to be treated in special ways. Otherwise, the dominant culture will continue to prevail to the detriment of diverse views.

4. Understand that culture counts more than structure. An educational institution recently went through a particularly traumatic time when the credibility of the administration was questioned by the faculty and staff. Various organizational consultants were interviewed to facilitate a healing process. Most of the consultants spoke of making the necessary structural changes to create a culture of trust. The consultant who was hired, however, began with the attitude that organizational structure has nothing to do with trust. Interpersonal relations based on mutual respect and an atmosphere of goodwill are what create a culture of trust. Would you rather work as part of a school with an outstanding reputation or work as part of a group of outstanding individuals? Many times these two characteristics are found in the same institution, but if one had to make a choice, my suspicion is that most people would opt to work with outstanding individuals.

So, it all starts with trust. These are exciting times in education. Revolutionary steps are being taken to restructure schools and rethink the teaching-learning process. Empowerment, total quality management, the use of technology, and strategic planning are becoming the norm in education. However, while these reforms have the potential to influence education in significantly positive ways, they must be based on a strong foundation to achieve their full potential.

Achieving educational effectiveness is an incremental, sequential improvement process. This process begins with the building of a sense of security within each individual so that he or she can be flexible in adapting to changes. Addressing only skills or techniques, such as communication, motivation, negotiation, or empowerment, is ineffective when individuals in an organization do not trust its systems, themselves, or each other. An institution's resources are wasted when invested only in training programs that assist administrators in mastering quick-fix techniques that, at best, attempt to manipulate employees and, at worst, reinforce mistrust.

The challenge is to transform the basis of relationships from insecurity, adversarialism, and politics into mutual trust. Trust is the beginning of effectiveness and forms the foundation of a principle-centered learning environment that emphasizes strengths and devises innovative methods to minimize weaknesses. The transformation process requires an internal locus of control that emphasizes individual responsibility and accountability for change and for promoting effectiveness. Of course, we argue that this transformation can be greatly facilitated by adopting the tenets of critical theory and the Ignatian tradition.

If one is expected to create a sense of trust and engender employee ownership of a change or reform, the change agent needs to be seen as making effective decisions. The administrative and organizational theory literature is in agreement about the two most important factors to be considered in determining the decision style that will produce the most effective decisions. While Vroom and Yetton's model includes the additional dimension of shared goals and conflict possibility, the two key elements are its quality, or the likelihood of one decision being more rational than another, and its acceptance, or the extent to which acceptance or commitment on the part of subordinates is crucial to its effective implementation.[11]

For example, if a new law is passed regarding the inclusion of special-education students, the quality of the decision (to promulgate it and include it in the catalog) is more important than the acceptance. Therefore, the appropriate decision style is command. That is, the administrator alone decides to promulgate it and include it in the catalog. In this case there is no need for participative decision making. On the other hand, if acceptance is more important than quality, or if the quality and acceptance are both important, as in the development of a new teacher evaluation instrument, the proper decision style is consensus. Finally, if neither the quality nor the acceptance is important, as in deciding, for instance, what color to paint the school lockers, convenience is the applicable style.

In addition to evaluating the quality and acceptance of a decision, one can assess how well it meets the criterion of ethical fairness and justice. Here is another instance where critical theory and the Ignatian vision come into play. Consider, for example, a disastrous decrease in standardized test scores in a high school. Top administrators are faced with the dilemma of whether to risk public outrage and the possible transfer of significant numbers of students or to gloss over the situation.

Administrators and staff can assess whether the decisions they make are ethical by applying personal moral codes or society's codes of values; they can apply philosophical views of ethical behavior; or they can assess the potential harmful consequences of behaviors to certain constituencies. One way of thinking about ethical decision making suggests that a person who makes a moral decision must first recognize the moral issue of whether a person's actions can hurt or help others; second, make a moral judgment; third, decide to attach greater priority to moral concerns than financial or other concerns, or establish their moral intent; and, finally, act on the moral concerns of the situation by engaging in moral behavior.[12] In conclusion, therefore, by combining the components of effective decision making with the characteristics of an ethical decision, the change agent can accomplish two important points: increase employee ownership of change, and build a culture of trust and respect.

Another issue that is important in developing ownership in the change process is the idea of empowerment. Empowering employees can have a motivating and energizing effect on their performance. Ironically, in the first wave of educational reforms in the 1980s teachers were identified as the problem. More recently, however, they have been identified as the solution. Critics of the early reforms argued that state-mandated educational standards and the prescribed content and form of schooling were too rigid to produce learners who can think critically, synthesize, and create new information.

The 1990s saw reform reports that brought a new focus to the challenges of improving American education. A bottom-up approach to reform was common among the most influential of these reports, which were produced by The Holmes Group, The Carnegie Forum, and The National Governors' Association.

The reports stressed that teachers have been assigned one of society's most difficult tasks, but have not been given the authority to perform it adequately. Effective teaching and learning consists of a complex mix of intellect, spontaneity, insight, personal understanding, love, and patience. Rules, especially those imposed from afar, constrain, rather than release, the learning process. The second wave of reform reports differed from the first by arguing that the restructuring should "empower teachers rather than manage them."

According to Thomas Sergiovanni and John Moore, empowerment is not the same as acknowledging the de facto discretion that already exists in the classroom. It is a deliberate effort to provide principals and teachers with the room, right, responsibility, and resources to make sensible decisions and informed professional judgments that reflect their circumstances. In effect, it gives basic education teachers the same type of academic freedom that those in higher education have.[13]

This effort calls for enhancing the professional status of teachers by providing them with more autonomy, training, trust, and collegial opportunities to carry out their tasks—that is, by not treating teachers like factory workers who are told what to do, how to do it, and when to do it. The effectiveness of this task-oriented approach is also being questioned in industry, by the way. The concept of empowerment has become a force in education, not only with teachers, but also with other educational personnel. Every school should be given the freedom and flexibility to respond creatively to its educational objectives and, above all, to meet the needs of its students. This approach engenders employee ownership and helps bring about change more effectively. It also coincides with the principles of critical theory and the Ignatian vision.

Diagnostic Checklist

Here are a few questions you can address in assessing whether you have created a sense of employee ownership in your institution:

- Are efforts made to establish a sense of trust and respect?
- Are the aspects of quality and acceptance being considered in the decision-making process?
- Is the appropriate decision-making style being used in a given situation?
- Is a sense of employee ownership being established and fostered?

PROVIDING STAFF DEVELOPMENT

Very often staff development, an essential part of the change process, is neglected or overlooked completely. Many educational reforms have failed because an enthusiastic leader has ill-advisedly tried to implement a change before engaging in staff development. Sometimes, even when staff development is provided, it has been ineffective. Negative responses to organized efforts in the name of staff development are the result of a history of poor experiences with activities that have taken place in the name of in-service training. However well-intended such activities may have been, too frequently they have not addressed the needs of the individual, the institution, or the nature of adult learners; invested the time and effort required; or recognized the importance of staff development to the ultimate success of any change or reform.

Staff development is a form of human-resource development, a process that uses developmental practices to bring about higher quality, greater productivity, and more satisfaction among employees as organization members. It is a function of an individual's knowledge, skills, and attitudes, together with the policies, structure, and management practices that make up the system in which the employee works. In a school setting, the ultimate goal of human-resource development is to produce the highest-quality instruction and service to the students.

The most important resource in an institution is its staff. When the staff's thinking is congruent with organizational needs, and when the staff is well-trained, adaptive, and motivated, effective schools result. To achieve this goal requires attention to the various ways in which human potential can be realized and to the variety of needs that any particular person and group may have at any particular stage of development.

The implications of critical theory and the Ignatian vision for staff development are widespread. In particular, Ignatius's concept of *cura personalis* (care of the person) is particularly applicable to staff development. Providing adequate and effective staff development enables individuals to reach their potential; it enables them to succeed. What better way is there to insure *cura personalis* than to provide a means for individuals to better actualize their potential? Effective staff development helps place individuals in such a position, and in doing so, manifests the Ignatian ideal of care of the person.

Diagnostic Checklist

Here are a few questions you can address in assessing the effectiveness of the staff development plan at your institution:

- Is a staff assessment and appraisal plan in effect?
- Is it used to develop a staff development plan?

- Are both group and individual development plans in effect?
- Is a mentoring system in effect?
- Is staff development part of the process of change at your institution?

OPERATIONALIZING CHANGE

Action follows identification of target forces for and against change, development of, selection of, and implementation of intervention strategies, and the determination of a staff-development plan. It is at this point that we operationalize the change, or give form to our vision. Although careful preparation for change increases the chances of success, it does not guarantee it. Placing the plan into operation requires establishment of the organizational structure that will best suit the change and development of an assessment process to determine if the change is remaining on course. Briefing sessions, special seminars, or other means of information dissemination must permeate the change effort. Operationalizing the change must include procedures for keeping all participants informed about the change activities and its effects.

The use of a broad-based steering committee to oversee the change may increase its likelihood of success. Such broad-based input is also in the critical theory and Ignatian traditions. This group, composed of representatives of all areas of the institution (external and internal), can advise on program budget and organizational policies and priorities. It is helpful if the same task force is active throughout the change process in that it provides needed continuity.

Further, the dynamic nature of organizational systems calls for flexibility in action. All efforts must include contingency plans for unanticipated costs, consequences, or resistance. A strong commitment to the change by top leaders can buffer change efforts from these difficulties and ensure the transfer of needed resources to the action plan.

Managing large-scale organizational change might require a more elaborate approach. The process includes at least four components:[14]

1. Pattern breaking involves freeing the system from structures, processes, and functions that are no longer useful. An organization

can be open to new options if it can relinquish approaches that no longer work or experience a paradigm shift.

2. Experimenting, by generating new patterns, encourages flexibility and yields new options. Training small groups of administrators to institute teamwork illustrates this element. To experiment, organizations must have a philosophy and mechanisms in place that encourage innovation and creativity and discourage coercion and fear of failure.

3. Visioning activities, such as building shared meaning throughout the institution and using the current mission statement, generate support for and commitment to the planned changes.

4. In the last component, bonding and attunement, management attempts to integrate all facets of the institutional change to move members toward the new way of action by focusing them on important tasks and generating constructive interpersonal relationships.

To operationalize a reform properly, the change agent needs to be keenly aware of the existing culture, the structure of the institution, and what form of organizational structure will best facilitate successful implementation of the change. For ease of operation, the various schools of thought regarding organizational structure can be grouped into three types of organizational theory, namely, classical organization theory, social-systems theory, and open-system theory. We related these theories to critical theory and the Ignatian vision in the previous chapter, but here we would like to discuss them in the context of the process of change.

CLASSICAL ORGANIZATION THEORY

The classical theorists believe that the application of bureaucratic structures and processes or organizational control will promote rational, efficient, and disciplined behavior, making possible the achievement of well-defined goals. Efficiency, then, is achieved by arranging positions within an organization according to hierarchy and jurisdiction and by placing power at the top of a clear chain of command. Scientific procedures also are used to determine the best way of performing a task, and then rules are formulated that require workers to perform in a prescribed manner. Experts are hired for defined roles and are grouped according to task specialization. Using rationally defined structures and processes such as these, a scientifically ordered flow of work can be carried out with maximum efficiency.

The conceptual model distilled from classical theory had a great impact on the practice and study of organizational life. It quickly spilled over the boundaries of industry and was incorporated into management practice in all sectors of society, including educational institutions. In fact, it is currently the dominant structural theory utilized in education. Thus, the tendency is to operationalize a change within the context of a classical structure. The obvious question is whether the classical structure lends itself effectively to all of the current reform movements. Critical theorists and humanists would answer that question with a resounding, "No!"

SOCIAL-SYSTEMS THEORY

Within the classical-theory framework, the individual worker was conceived of as an object, a part of the bureaucratic machine. Preparing the work environment for maximizing labor efficiency was not unlike applying precepts from the physical sciences to the human domain of work. As Elton Mayo found in the Hawthorne Works' studies, the impact of social-psychological variables within a worker group was significant. The discovery that workers could control the production process to a considerable degree, independently of the demands of management, shattered many of the precepts central to classical theory. A new era of organizational theory, and one more in tune with critical theory and the Ignatian vision, had arrived. This domain of thought is sometimes referred to as social-systems theory.[15]

Classical management theory taught that the needs of the organization and the needs of the worker coincided—if the company prospered, the worker prospered as well. However, as an awareness of the basic differences between the needs of the individual and the needs of the organization grew, and as worker groups became more sophisticated in manipulating the production process, management technology gave birth to social-systems theory and its approaches as a means of reducing conflict. The argument went that by being considerate, using democratic procedures whenever possible, and maintaining open lines of communication, management and workers could talk over their respective problems and resolve them in a friendly, congenial way.

Once again, the philosophy behind the new approach to management—this time the human-relations orientation to the problems of managerial control—quickly spread to other sectors of society, including education. The social upheaval caused by the Depression and the turmoil of World War II created a receptive climate for this new administrative theory. Enthusiasm for the human-relations orientation dampened considerable after the 1950s, however, because many worker organizations came to view it as just another management tactic designed to exploit workers.

The study of behavior in social-systems settings intensified, however, and a greater sophistication developed about how and why group members behave as they do under given conditions. In time, a natural social-systems orientation to the analysis of behavior evolved in the literature as an alternative to the rational-systems approach. The natural social-systems orientation attempts to take into account how people do behave in organizations, rather than how they should behave.

The conceptual perspective of the natural social-systems model suggests that an organization consists of a collection of groups (social systems) that collaborate to achieve system goals on some occasions and goals of their own groups on other occasions. Coalitions among subgroups within an organization (e.g. English teachers, history teachers, and biology teachers) form to provide power bases on which action can be taken (e.g., "Let's all vote to reject writing behavioral objectives"). Within the social-systems framework, the study of formal and informal power is one of several critical variables used to identify and analyze the processes of organizational governance.

OPEN-SYSTEM THEORY

During the 1960s, another strand of thought developed that originated in the new technostructure of society. The earlier two traditions of classical and social-systems theory tended to view organizational life as a closed system—that is, as isolated from the surrounding environment. Open-system theory sees an organization as a set of interrelated parts that interact with the environment. It receives inputs, such as human and material resources, values, community expectations, and societal demands; transforms them through a production process (e.g., classroom activities); and exports the product (e.g., graduates, new knowledge, revised value sets) into the environment (e.g., businesses, the military, homes, and colleges) with value added. The organization receives a return (e.g., community financial support in the form of school taxes or tuition) for its efforts so it can survive and prosper and begin the cycle over again.

Within the open-system theory context, the organization is perceived as consisting of cycles of events that interlock through exporting and importing with other organizations, which also are made up of cycles of events. Management is very complex because leadership has almost no control over the shifting conditions in the environment (e.g., new laws, demographic shifts, political climate, market for graduates) on the input or output side of the equation. Control of the production process is also complex because the various subsystems of the organization (e.g., athletic department or minority-group students) are also shaped by event cycles that are programmed by values, expectations, traditions, and vested interests. Changing these internal subgroups and their event cycles is difficult. The administrator attempts to stream the cycles together so that minimum conflict and inefficiency is generated.

Through the perspective of open-system theory, a new logic on issues of organizational governance has emerged. It emphasizes the relationship of the organization with its surrounding environment and, thus, places a premium on planning and programming events that cannot be controlled directly. The key to making an open system work effectively and efficiently is harnessing its ability to gather, process, and use information. In a school, the facility with which a need is discovered, a goal is established, and resources are coalesced to meet that need determines the effectiveness and efficiency of that school. This characteristic of the institution is particularly important if change is to take place effectively.

CONTINGENCY THEORY

In recent years, a view of organization development has surfaced that treats each organization, and even entities within the organization, as unique. For centuries this orientation has been at the core of practitioner behavior, but seen as anomalous, reflective of inefficiency or unpreparedness (managing by the seat of your pants), and thus overlooked by management scientists. Currently, the changing situational character of management is now coming to be understood as a key to the management process itself.

Many management scholars and practitioners would now agree that contingency theory is perhaps the most powerful current and future trend in organizational development. At this stage, however, contingency theory is not really a theory. Rather, it is a conceptual tool that facilitates our understanding of the situational flow of events and alternate organizational and individual responses to that flow. Thus, as a conceptual tool, contingency theory does not possess the holistic character of the three major models discussed earlier. In many ways, contingency theory can be thought of as a subset of open-system theory because it is through open-system theory that we come to understand the dynamic flows of events, personnel, and resources that take place in organizations. It is also helpful for understanding the process of change and the need for the educational institution undergoing change to have facets of all three mainstream organizational structures. It is equally important that the change agent be aware of the impact on the organizational structure of whether the reform is ultimately implemented successfully.

IMPLEMENTING THE PLAN

Critical theory and the Ignatian vision would suggest that aspects of the social-systems theory be utilized wherever possible. However, contingency theory would suggest that the best aspects of all of the structural theories be utilized in appropriate situations. Nevertheless, once the organizational structure is in place, the next step in operationalizing the change is to devise and implement a plan of action. The reform project should be separated into a series of activities, with the complex activities being subdivided into elements or events, the completion of which will conclude the activity. Clearly defined responsibilities should be assigned and accepted. Before proceeding, there is need to establish realistic target dates, develop the project calendar, and put into place a monitoring and evaluation process. Project-planning computer software is of great assistance in organizing and managing large projects.[16]

Diagnostic Checklist

Here are a few questions you can address in assessing your institution's readiness to operationalize a change:

- Has the organizational structure of your institution been analyzed?
- Is an appropriate organizational structure in place?
- If not, can one be developed?
- Are the best aspects of the various organizational models being utilized?
- Are characteristics of the open-system and the contingency models of organizational structure present?

EVALUATING CHANGE

The next step in the integrated change process is the evaluation of the change. Authentic assessment is a topical issue in education these days. Many are asking how to assess performance most accurately, effectively, and fairly. After generations of focusing on program inputs, stressing program outcomes as an authentic measure of a program's effectiveness is gaining in popularity. The emphasis on outcomes should be applied to the evaluation of a change or reform.

The change agent(s) should collect data about the nature and effectiveness of the change. The results of the evaluation indicate whether the change process is complete or a return to an earlier stage should occur. The criteria for success should be specified in advance of a change effort. These criteria may be culturally linked and varied; they should also be closely related to the goals of the reform. If ineffective outcomes result from the introduction of site-based management, for example, the process should return to an earlier stage, such as assessment, to determine if the institution is really in need of it and the school community has been properly prepared.

One process for evaluating the effectiveness of a change or reform is to consider participants' affective reactions, learning, behavior changes, and performance changes.[17] Affective reactions are the participants' attitudes or disposition toward the reform. Questionnaires and interviews can be used to collect this information. Obviously, the change agent is looking for development of a positive attitude toward the change. If it has been operationalized successfully, positive attitudes should prevail.

Learning refers to the participants' understanding of the change and the acquisition of new knowledge and skills as a result of its successful implementation. In the case of introducing cooperative learning techniques in the classroom, for example, did the participants develop an understanding of the principles of cooperative learning, and do they demonstrate the skills needed to implement it properly in the classroom? Classroom observations are one way of assessing whether appropriate learning has taken place. If the staff-development phase of the integrated change process has been implemented properly, appropriate learning should be apparent.

Behavioral changes include participants' actions in the workplace. Do they interact appropriately with colleagues and others? The following behaviors might result from an effectively implemented change:

- Communicating openly. This includes sharing intentions, motives, needs, feelings, and observations; asking for and giving feedback that is descriptive, rather than judgmental, and specific, rather than general; using active-listening techniques, such as paraphrasing, summarizing, asking for clarification, and monitoring one's external behavior and attitude; using assertive-communication techniques, rather than being nonassertive or aggressive.
- Collaborating. This includes discussing, planning, and revising the goals of the reform jointly and cooperatively; using participative decision-making techniques and avoiding arbitrary and unilateral decisions; expanding influence skills so that compelling arguments for one's point of view can be made, rather than making decisions by fiat.
- Taking responsibility. This includes being a self-starter and not depending on constant direction; taking the initiative to develop innovative and creative ways of performing one's duties; streamlining the organization or department activities to promote operating efficiency.
- Maintaining a shared vision. This includes developing and communicating a clear philosophy, along with goals and objectives;

having and telling a story, a shared history that gives meaning to the institution's activities; creating rituals and ceremonies to reestablish and remember values.

- Solving problems effectively. This includes defining problems in a nonadversarial way so that they may be resolved from a win-win perspective, rather than a win-lose one; perceiving and projecting problems as challenges, rather than obstacles; using group problem-solving techniques where applicable.
- Respecting/supporting. This involves using the various motivational theories to generate enthusiasm and affirm and support desired behavior; dwelling on an individual's strengths, rather than on his or her weaknesses; giving individuals the benefit of the doubt, and not being judgmental; exhibiting ethical behavior and treating everyone fairly; in other words, displaying the outcomes of practicing critical theory and the Ignatian vision.
- Processing/facilitating interactions. This includes clarifying meeting goals and purposes; reserving time at the end of meetings to critique what was done well and poorly, what facilitated decision making or performing the task (a colleague of mine ends every meeting by asking each individual, "What did you learn today?" While this can be annoying if overdone, it is an effective example of processing/facilitating interactive behavior).
- Inquiring and experimenting. This includes using an analytical approach to problem solving, and in the process, looking for new and creative ways of addressing an issue; frequently examining and questioning the existing structure and culture to be certain they maximize the institution's goals.

The following are common behavior changes that educational leaders exhibit when a change or reform has been operationalized properly:

- Generating participation. This includes involving other people when they have the necessary expertise, when the decision must be high in quality, and when it also requires high acceptance; relaxing traditional lines of command and empowering others to make decisions; assuming a delegating, coaching style, rather than a directive, task-oriented style.

- Leading with vision. This includes continually articulating the institution's mission, goals, and objectives; providing feedback mechanisms whereby faculty and staff know the institutions' goals; revising the institution's mission and the leader's personal vision when necessary.
- Functioning strategically. This includes articulating underlying causes, interdependencies, and long-range consequences and acting accordingly; acting in an institutional mode, rather than a territorial one; developing strategies and tactics to operationalize the institution's mission and goals; developing among the faculty and staff the knowledge and skills required to meet future objectives.
- Promoting information flow. This includes communicating clearly the elements necessary to make the change effective; being clear about expectations, commitments, and needs; establishing multiple channels of communication and using the appropriate one under existing circumstances; establishing the proper chain of command for the various types of communication (e.g., external communication ordinarily should follow a formal chain of command, while internal communication may follow a less formal, matrix line); enhancing mechanisms for feedback.
- Developing others. This is where critical theory and the Ignatian vision once again apply and includes teaching needed skills and preparing others within the institution to replace those who may leave; rewarding desired behavior and delegating to those who prove ready and capable of increased responsibility; providing opportunities for and building on employees' success; adapting one's leadership style to the readiness level of followers.

EVALUATING INSTITUTIONAL CHANGE

In evaluating the effectiveness of an institutional reform and the process leading to the change, an institution may address the following questions:[18]

- How did the institution determine the knowledge and skills necessary to implement the reform, and what type of staff-development program was used to bring about the desired results?

- What were the conditions—economic, political, and demographic—of the external environment at the time of the reform?
- Did the conditions in the external environment have an effect on the success of the reform?
- How much has the institution's internal environment changed, and has that changed the effectiveness of the reform?
- What are the primary technologies necessary to implement the reform?
- Is the division of labor appropriate to implement the change.
- What is the prevailing norm of the institution regarding improvement efforts?
- How comprehensive and consistent with current organizational theory were the guiding assumptions and models used in implementing the reform?
- Were the urgency and ends of the reform clear and accepted?
- Was a change process established, and were all of the steps used and integrated?
- Were the appropriate change agents identified and empowered?
- How explicit and detailed were the plans?
- What were the intended outcomes of the program, and what were the actual outcomes?
- How were the outcomes assessed?

The answers to these questions will enable the evaluator to assess whether the reform attained its objectives and, if it did not, to determine the possible reasons.

Diagnostic Checklist

Here are a few questions you can address in assessing your institution's evaluation process:

- Is an evaluation process an integral part of the change process?
- Does the evaluation process use authentic assessment devices?
- Is the evaluation process outcomes-based?
- Are the outcomes related to the reform's goals?

- Is there a mechanism for revising the reform if evaluation of the outcomes indicates that revision is appropriate?

INSTITUTIONALIZING CHANGE

Provided that the evaluation process shows that the reform has been effective, the change should then become institutionalized—that is, the changed processes should be established as permanent ways of operating. Otherwise, when the current change agent leaves, the change may not be perpetuated. Ideally, the reform should become part of the organizational culture. It is in this way that a legacy is created from which future generations of students, parents, faculty, and staff can benefit. The results of a failure to institutionalize a reform are often seen at the state and federal Department of Education levels. How many times have we seen a governor or president set an educational agenda, only for it to be scuttled and replaced with a different agenda by the subsequent administration? If a successful change is to prevail over time, it must be institutionalized.

Thus, action must extend beyond short-term changes for real organizational improvement to take place. Enculturating the change must be a significant goal of the integrated change process. How, for example, does a reform like site-based management become a permanent part of the governance structure of a school? Certainly the way the activities are performed in moving from the first to the last step in the integrated change process will influence the permanency of the change. Accurate targeting of forces influencing change, followed by careful selection of change agents and intervention strategies, concluding with effective action all contribute to long-range improvement.

In addition, mechanisms for continual monitoring of the changes must be developed and instituted. Permanent committees or task forces to observe ongoing implementation and outcomes can serve the monitoring functions. Formulation of new institutional policies and procedures based on the reform can encourage its continuation. Most important, however, is a commitment to the reform by the great majority of the school community. This community's commitment will expedite the reform's institutionalization.

Educational leaders, therefore, must build learning communities that emphasize ongoing adaptability and self-generation, thereby emphasizing coping and looking at the world creatively. Peter Senge says, "Leaders in learning organizations are responsible for building organizations where people are continually expanding their capabilities to shape their future—that is, leaders are responsible for learning."[19] Where better to implement Senge's ideas regarding a learning community than in an educational institution?

Another way of institutionalizing a reform is by encouraging the development of "heroes" who embody the institution's vision and "tribal storytellers" who promulgate it. We often hear individuals in various organizations describe a colleague as "an institution around here." Heroes such as these do more to establish the organizational culture of an institution than any manual or handbook of policies and procedures ever written. The senior faculty member who is recognized and respected for his or her knowledge and human treatment of students is an invaluable asset to an educational institution. This person is a symbol of the institution's character. It is the presence of these heroes that sustains the reputation of the institution and allows workers to feel good about themselves and about the place where they work. The deeds and accomplishments of these heroes need to be promulgated to become part of the institution's folklore.

The deeds of these heroes are usually perpetuated by an organization's tribal storytellers, individuals who know the history of the institution and relate it through stories of its former and current heroes. An effective leader encourages the tribal storytellers, knowing that they are serving an invaluable service. They work at the process of institutional renewal; they allow the institution to improve continuously; they preserve and revitalize the values of the institution; and they mitigate the tendency of institutions, especially educational institutions, to become bureaucratic. Every institution has its heroes and storytellers. It is the educational leader's function to see to it that things like manuals and handbooks do not replace them.

One caveat regarding these heroes and storytellers, however, is that they can also perpetuate the status quo and, thus, be a force against change. The key is to let them know first about a change to be implemented. If informed at the outset and convinced of the reform's efficacy, the heroes and storytellers can be among the change agent's most valuable assets throughout the process, especially during the institutionalization phase. Cultivation of heroes and storytellers needs to take place early in the process if they are to be an asset by the end of the process. This is yet another indication of the importance of considering this process as integrated, rather than step-by-step.

Diagnostic Checklist

Here are a few questions you can address in assessing whether your institution has institutionalized a change:

- Has the evaluation process indicated that the change has been effective?
- Has the foundation been established by involving the heroes and storytellers early in the process?
- Has the change been incorporated into the institution's catalogs, manuals, and handbooks?
- Have the heroes and storytellers been encouraged to participate in institutionalizing the change?

NOTES

1. E. Mark Hanson, *Educational Administration and Organizational Behavior* (Boston: Allyn and Bacon, 1991).

2. Max de Pree, *Leadership Is an Art*, (New York: Dell Publishing, 1989).

3. E. Mark Hanson, *Educational Administration and Organizational Behavior* (Boston: Allyn and Bacon, 1991).

4. Richard Carlson, "Barriers to Change in Public Schools," in *Change Processor in Public Schools*, Richard Carlson et al. (eds.) (Eugene: University of Oregon, Center for the Advanced Study of Educational Administration, 1965).

5. Goodwin Watson, "Resistance to Change," in *The Planning of Change*, Warren Bennis et al. (eds.) (New York: Holt, Rinehart, and Winston, 1969) p. 488.

6. Herbert A. Simon, *The New Science of Management Decision* (New York: Harper & Row, 1960).

7. Michael G. Fullan, "Coordinating Top-Down and Bottom-Up Strategies for Educational Reform," *The Governance of Curriculum Journal* 28 (1995): 30–48.

8. S. Sarason, *The Predictable Failure of Educational Reform* (San Francisco: Jossey-Bass, 1990).

9. S. Sarason, *The Predictable Failure of Educational Reform* (San Francisco: Jossey-Bass, 1990).

10. D. Taylor and C. Teddlie, "Restructuring and the Classroom: A View from a Reform District," paper presented at the Annual Meeting of the American Education Research Association, San Francisco, 1992.

11. V. H. Vroom and P. W. Yetton, *Leadership and Decision Making* (Pittsburgh: University of Pittsburgh Press, 1973).

12. Robert H. Palestini, *Educational Administration: Leading With Mind and Heart* (Lancaster: Technomic Publishing, 1999).

13. Thomas J. Sergiovanni and John H. Moore, *Schooling for Tomorrow* (Boston: Allyn and Bacon, 1988).

14. David A. Nadler, *Champions of Change* (San Francisco: Jossey-Bass, 1990).

15. Judith R. Gordon, *Organizational Behavior*, 4th ed. (Boston: Allyn and Bacon, 1993).

16. Robert H. Palestini, *Ten Steps to Educational Reform* (Lanham, MD: Scarecrow Press, 2000).

17. David A. Nadler, *Champions of Change* (San Francisco: Jossey-Bass, 1990).

18. Petra Snowden and Richard Gorton, *School Leadership and Administration*, 6th ed. (New York: McGraw-Hill, 2002).

19. Peter Senge, "The Leader's New Work: Building Learning Organizations," *Sloan Management Review* (Fall 1990): 7–23.

CHAPTER 8

Educational Choice and Vouchers: A Case Study

Economic inequality in the United States is growing, and it threatens to tear the heart out of our civil society. Given the faith Americans have always placed in education as an engine of material and cultural progress, schools will inevitably be asked to play an ethical role in reversing this destructive trend.

This text examines our role as educators in providing an opportunity in our schools and in our classrooms for all children to succeed—not just the white children, not just the brightest children, not only well-behaved students, not only socioeconomically advantaged students, but all students. Inclusion, as defined here, is the Ignatian and critical view that there is an ethical responsibility on our part to provide all young people with real and equal access to a quality education; anything else is the politics of exclusion. Let us, then, use a consideration of school choice in the form of educational vouchers as a case study and examine its viability through the lens of critical theory and the Ignatian vision.

Despite the many arguments that diminish the rationale behind school choice, I would suggest that one important way of ensuring that all children have the opportunity to achieve would be for each state to consider implementing a school-choice program funded by educational tuition vouchers. I know that a notion such as this is considered to be heresy by many in the so-called public-school establishment. Many of its opponents characterize school choice as the strategy of neoconservatives (the structural-functionalists and positivists) to exploit the dissatisfaction of poor, predominantly minority parents who have been left behind by our economy in order to achieve the goal of creating a publicly funded private-school system free of public control and oversight. If achieved, they say, this alternative system will inevitably reproduce and legally sanction the doctrine of "separate but equal" on a grand scale, with the primary beneficiaries being middle- and upper-middle-class families. In other words, the politics of private-school choice now resembles a high-stakes version of the old bait-and-switch scam.[1] Unfortunately, such ad hominum, strident, and inflammatory arguments are too often the knee-jerk reactions of many of the school-choice protagonists.

I would venture to say that most members of the public-school establishment, as well as many academics, consider voucher plans to be exclusionary, rather than inclusionary, and believe that, if implemented, they would ultimately render the public schools the educators of the lowest strata of our society. Such a view contradicts our limited experience with educational vouchers. The reality is that a well-crafted system of educational vouchers, awarded according to economic need and physical and mental disability, could serve as a vehicle for inclusion that would enable many of the most underserved students in our society to choose a school that they and their parents consider to be superior. And, because of the introduction of some healthy competition, all schools, including the public schools, may benefit.

The suggested voucher plan would be limited to a relatively small group of young people whose families are economically disadvantaged or have a child with physical or mental disabilities. Thus, such a plan would not have a significant negative impact on public-school enrollment. The Milwaukee and the Cleveland Plans come immediately to mind as examples of how such a system could work, although none of these models includes vouchers for those who have physical or mental disabilities. The outcomes of both the Milwaukee and Cleveland voucher plans have been positive, and neither city has experienced a significant decline in public-school enrollment or any of the other Armageddon-like consequences that many have predicted.[2] Furthermore, it is interesting to note that until recently, the great majority of the countries in the world that have government dollars going exclusively to public or state schools were communist, or other types of dictatorships, while the great majority of the democratic countries in the world provide government aid to a variety of schools, including private schools. I believe that it is time to reconsider our current monolithic paradigm whereby only public schools are funded through tax dollars.

In exploring this topic, we will consider three perspectives: the market-economy model, the liberal or Ignatian tradition, and the critical pedagogy model. The market-driven model is most concerned with efficiency of operation. Its theorists might ask, how can we deliver education and achieve the biggest bang for our buck? Those in the liberal tradition are concerned with equality. They might ask, how can we ensure that every student has an equal opportunity to achieve? The critical pedagogues are concerned with social justice and inclusion. They might ask, how can we structure our educational systems so that the least privileged and the least powerful are not marginalized?

THE THEORETICAL DEVELOPMENT OF SCHOOL CHOICE

Assuming some level of government financing, the school-choice issue comes down to this: Should students be assigned to schools based upon politically established criteria, or should they be able to choose the schools they will attend? Any answer must contain qualifications and caveats. The following is a review of several influential school-choice proposals and the accompanying rationales given for greater reliance on markets and democratic principles for providing education. In my conclusion, I will relate my recommendations and observations concerning one or more of these theories or rationales.

THE MARKET-ECONOMY MODEL

Milton Friedman's market-economy voucher model has been enormously influential.[3] The market-economy model posits that education should be subjected to the exigencies of supply and demand, just as most other products and services in a capitalistic country are. Friedman reasoned that in a society based on voluntary cooperation, all individuals must have a basic level of education. Friedman admitted that it is difficult to determine precisely where the public benefits of education stop and the private benefits begin. Yet, because there is a public benefit to education, he argued that some public action should be taken to ensure the adequate education of all members of society. Because of noncompliance problems, Friedman said this action must involve more than setting school-attendance rules. Hence, he proposed that subsidies be provided to those families that could not cover the costs of educating their children.

Friedman next noted that while government financing and provision of education are typically combined, they could and should be separated. The financing function should be achieved by giving subsidies to families through educational vouchers to purchase a specified minimum amount of education per child per year, if spent on approved educational services. Friedman suggested that parents be free to spend the voucher amount and any additional amount on the school of their choice. Further, education could be supplied by a range of organizations, including for-profit firms and nonprofit institutions. The government's role in providing education, rather than financing it, would be restricted to upholding minimum standards, including, perhaps, the teaching of some minimum common content.

Having made this proposal, Freidman defended it against potential criticisms. Where decentralized decision making could lead to the same outcome as centralized decision making, Friedman argued that the decentralized route should be taken for two reasons. First, the use of collective decision making tends to strain the social cohesion essential for a stable society. Second, government decision making requires that once decisions are made, people conform to them, even if they disagree. As well as potentially engendering ill feeling, this requirement to conform also stifles innovation. Friedman argued that a system of education vouchers would allow greater individual decision making and create competition among educational institutions, a powerful force for promoting innovative schooling practices.

Friedman's proposal was fairly simple. Rather than elaborating on the details of such an approach, he chose to show that many of the arguments that could be made against it could just as easily be made against the present system of schooling. For example, Friedman argued that it is disingenuous to claim that vouchers will exacerbate class distinction. In looking at the present organization of education in society, we find that there is much stratification, even when schooling is produced primarily in the public sector. Thus, Friedman claimed:

Under present arrangements, stratification of residential areas effectively restricts the intermingling of children from decidedly different backgrounds. In addition, parents are not now prevented from sending their children to private schools. Only a highly limited class can or does do so, parochial schools aside, thus producing further stratification."[4]

Friedman concluded that the present school system appears to promote inequality, and he saw this as a serious problem that makes it all the harder for the exceptional few, who are the hope of the future, to rise above the poverty of their initial state.

THE LIBERAL TRADITION

A number of educational theorists are uncomfortable with Friedman's model because they observed that when individuals are left to their own devices in determining their behavior, oftentimes, prejudices and discrimination surface. Those theorists in the liberal tradition were concerned about equal opportunity and equity of treatment.

The liberal tradition started with sociologist Christopher Jencks, who suggested that private schools could help to remedy educational problems in the inner city. I would argue that it started with Ignatius of Loyola more than 450 years earlier. Nonetheless, a veteran teacher, Mario Fantini, wrote a book on alternative public schools in which he argued for the use of vouchers within the public-school system. Education academics John Coons and Stephen Sugarman argued for the use of vouchers to address equity concerns.[5]

Jencks was motivated by the perilous state of inner-city public schools. In his view, the problems facing these schools originated from the overly bureaucratic nature of the systems they operated within and the low pay levels of teachers and administrators. In combination, Jencks argued, this has led to the creation of a system of education whose first axiom is that everyone, on every level, is incompetent and irresponsible. As a result, innovative ideas are very unlikely to emerge from the lower ranks in the hierarchy, and top-down reforms become difficult to implement.

In developing his argument, Jencks suggested that government-financed education vouchers, or tuition grants, combined with private-school provision, would have two major benefits. First, private control would make it possible to attack management problems. Second, the use of tuition grants would put an end to neighborhood schools. Jencks believed that education involves interacting with others from a variety of socioeconomic backgrounds. However, the neighborhood schools with their specified attendance zones prevent this sort of mixing. Jencks admitted that these actions would destroy the public-school system. In response to this, he said, "we must not allow the memory of past achievements to blind us to present failures."

Having developed this theoretical justification for school choice, in association with his colleagues from the Center for the Study of Public Policy at Harvard, Jencks went on to design a voucher system to transform inner-city schooling. This work led to the Alum Rock, California, experiment, which is discussed later. In contrast to Friedman's relatively simple, straightforward voucher plan, Jencks' plan was very complex. In an effort in ensure equal opportunity and equity, Jencks' plan contained rules for how applicants could choose their schools, how schools could choose their applicants, and how lottery systems would operate in cases of oversubscription.

Another theorist in the liberal tradition, Mario Fantini, extended the discussion of the ways that education vouchers could promote innovation.[6] He contrasted himself with Friedman and Jencks by arguing that the public-school system could reform itself and ensure equal opportunity and equity. Fantini called for an "internal voucher" that would allow real alternatives to emerge within the public-school system. Fantini did not want vouchers to apply to nonpublic schools for fear that low-quality schools would emerge. The Minnesota public-school voucher plan, which will be discussed later, operationalized many of Fantini's principles.

Fantini's model was designed to give parents, students, and teachers a choice among alternative types of schools. He suggested a "house" concept, whereby schools would be subdivided into houses for science, foreign languages, humanities, and the like, so that greater individual attention could be given. According to some, Fantini stands alone in making an education-inspired case for school choice. Although his work received a wide amount of interest within education circles at the time it was published, Fantini is rarely cited in contemporary debates. But his ideas influenced individuals who have become important voices in the school-choice debate.

Also in the liberal tradition, John Coons and S. D. Sugarman took as their starting point the observation that a just society must provide the formal portion of a child's education.[7] They placed primary emphasis on promoting educational equity. This rendered their plan for school choice complicated because of the substantial differences in income among individuals in American society. According to Coons and Sugarman, educational vouchers needed to differ in amount depending on family income and on the tuition charges at the chosen school. Unlike previous theoretical work on school-choice approaches, this approach required extensive data on family size and income in order to be implemented. Thus, in an effort to ensure equity, the process became administratively cumbersome.

In 1990, The Brookings Institute published John Chubb and Terry Moe's *Politics, Markets, and America's Schools*, a book central to recent school-choice debates. In it they combined the market-economy theory with that of the liberal tradition. They believed that their voucher rationale was operationalized in the Harlem District 4 experiment, which will be discussed in more detail later.

Chubb and Moe, both political scientists, took as their starting point the observation that, by most accounts, the American education system is not working well. They took an organizational-development approach to analyzing the problem and concluded that the institutional arrangements that have evolved in public schools make them unresponsive and ineffective.

In their empirical work, Chubb and Moe built upon the finding of James Coleman that school autonomy was the single most important element in the success of schools in academic achievement.[8] Based on these findings, Chubb and Moe asserted that bureaucracy is unambiguously problematic for school organization. But bureaucracy is an essential for democratic control. Therefore, Chubb and Moe concluded that because the institutions of democratic control work systematically and powerfully to discourage school autonomy, in turn they discourage school effectiveness. If public schools are to become more effective, the institutions that control them must be changed. To improve American schools, they proposed a new system, eliminating centralized bureaucracies and vesting authority directly in the hands of schools, parents, and students.

THE CRITICAL-PEDAGOGY PERSPECTIVE

The critical-pedagogy perspective grows out of the strongly held belief that schooling cannot be separated from the social context within which it takes place. Thus, a discourse on ethics, the distribution of power, and the plight of the underserved must be included in any debate on how education should be delivered.[9] Critical pedagogues decry the current heavy emphasis on testing to assess academic achievement. Thus, any notion of educational choice that develops out of a disparity of test scores between public and non-public-school students is very problematic. Those espousing this perspective would posit that, in this context, school choice is organized and developed according to the logic and imperatives of the marketplace. Ignoring the primacy of the social, choice appeals to the logic of competitiveness, individualism, and achievement. While these attributes might sound plausible as fundamental elements in the logic of educational reform, they, in fact, are used by neoconservatives like Milton Friedman to develop a notion of educational leadership that undermines the responsibility of public service, ruptures the relationship between schools and the community, and diverts educators from improving education in all schools.

These theorists are also alarmed that the new educational reform movements, including school choice, refuse to develop a deeper critical moral discourse. More specifically, missing from the current neoconservative emphasis on educational reform is a discourse that can illuminate what administrators, teachers, and other cultural workers actually do in terms of the underlying principles and values that structure the stories, visions, and experiences that inform school and classroom practices. The current discourse offers few insights into how schools should prepare students to push against the oppressive boundaries of gender, class, race, and age domination. Nor does it provide the language for students to investigate the ways in which questions and matters concerning the curriculum are really struggles concerning issues of self-identity, culture, power, and history. In effect, the crisis of authority is grounded in a refusal to address how particular forms of authority are secured and legitimized at the expense of cultural democracy, critical citizenship, and basic human rights. By refusing to interrogate the values that not only frame how authority is constructed, but also define leadership as a political and pedagogical practice, neoconservative educational reformers end up subordinating the discourse of ethics to the rules of management and efficiency.

Despite these concerns, however, there are critical pedagogy theorists who posit that a well-crafted choice plan that takes into consideration the aforementioned concerns could be effective. Herbert Gintis, a neo-Marxist, is one such theorist. He contends that the analysis of the competitive delivery of educational services has often been couched in terms of an opposition between government regulation and the free market. However, regulation and the free market may be complementary and, under appropriate conditions, interact as a context for cost-effective, egalitarian, and socially accountable education.[10] The government must provide some services on a monopolistic basis because competitive delivery of these services may be excessively costly. Tax collection, police protection, national defense, and other regulatory agencies are examples. In each case, one could make a compelling argument that competitive delivery would not be effective. In the case of education, however, it would be more difficult to make such a compelling argument. In fact, unless there are structural forces prohibiting the emergence of effective regulation, or the costs of efficient regulation are excessively high, competitive delivery of educational services should better meet the private needs of parents and children, while fulfilling the educational system's traditional social functions as well.

Gintis maintains that the public expects schools to teach certain skills: reading, writing, history, math, and science, punctuality and self-discipline. If they are dissatisfied with the results of what they are getting, it would be advantageous to them to be able to leverage their dissatisfaction in support of change by threatening to take their business elsewhere. The existing public-school establishment disempowers parents by obliging them to utilize a Byzantine governance system to effect change. The competitive delivery of educational services, properly funded and regulated, might succeed in expediting and circumventing this cumbersome process.

Educators, on the other hand, have higher expectations for education. In addition to reading, writing, and arithmetic, they expect schools to promote equality and tolerance, teach artistic, aesthetic and spiritual values, and create community. The concept that these ideals can be promoted in a marketplace model is repugnant to many, but this need not be the case if the school-choice program is properly crafted. The choice of educational goals can still be debated in the political arena, and the results could be implemented through the proper choice of policy tools, which would be codified in the rules for funding and accrediting schools. The use of the market is in this sense an instrument of, rather than an alternative to, democratic policy making.[11]

SCHOOL CHOICE AND THE IGNATIAN VISION

Earlier, we explored five of the beliefs that embody the Ignatian vision: the *magis* principle, *cura personalis*, discernment, service to others, and social justice. Looking at school choice and educational vouchers through the lens of the Ignatian vision, one can easily observe how these five beliefs are manifested.

It seems clear that the monolithic system of American public education has not served all of our young people well. Its deficiencies are most apparent in the urban and rural areas where most children come from poverty-stricken environments. In continually seeking the more (*magis*), the Ignatian vision would encourage us to find a better way of doing things. Educational vouchers may provide us with this better way. However, whether vouchers constitute a better way needs to be observed under the microscope of the other Ignatian principles enumerated above. Do vouchers serve the individual (*cura personalis*) in a better way? Are they the best alternative currently available (discernment)? Do they serve the community, especially the poor and disenfranchised (service and social justice)?

Certainly the current system of public education does not allow for individual differences. Its very foundation is based on the concept that one size fits all. The government funds only public schools, even if parents believe that their tax dollars should be invested in an alternative to public schools. By its nature, therefore, a public-education monopoly does not have the care of the individual as its focus. Rather, it is the care of society that is its focus. Educational vouchers, on the other hand, would allow parents to determine which type of education best meets the needs of their particular children, whether it be provided by a public or a nonpublic school. And, we will demonstrate that such an arrangement will also benefit society at large.

In discerning the various alternatives available to us regarding the education of our young people, it seems that school choice may be the most viable and effective. However, as we have seen, there are a variety of school-choice approaches available. Even if school choice seems preferable to our nation's current education policy, which of the school-choice plans is the most equitable and viable? To answer this question, we need to discern which of the alternatives would serve society the best and ultimately lead to equality of educational opportunity and social justice.

If school vouchers were made equally available to all parents, as Milton Friedman and others have suggested, equality would be achieved, but to the detriment of equity or fairness. Providing vouchers to parents who can already afford educational alternatives seems wasteful and unjust. A more equitable plan would be one in the liberal or critical-pedagogue tradition, which would provide vouchers to those who were the most financially or physically needy. Thus, in order to reflect the Ignatian vision, a voucher plan sensitive to and available to only the most underserved and marginalized would be acceptable. In my conclusion, I suggest such a plan.

A CASE FOR SCHOOL CHOICE

The rather widespread and growing appeal of school choice may be attributed to several key factors. First, on average, non-public-school students outperform their public-school counterparts in terms of standardized achievement test scores, graduation rates, and the probability of attending college. Proponents of school choice argue that these results can be explained by the greater efficiency of nonpublic schools, which do not have the bloated bureaucracy and rigid set of policies that impede good teaching and learning and make public schools less effective. However, an alternative explanation is that differences in performance between students in public and nonpublic schools can be explained by differences in school resources or in the backgrounds of students. For instance, non-public-school students tend to come from better-educated families with above-average incomes. It seems likely, opponents of school choice argue, that these factors would contribute to a good educational environment in the home. Still, the fact that private-school students generally outperform their public-school counterparts lends credence to the notion that nonpublic schools are doing a better job of educating students than are public schools.

Second, vouchers would give more control over educational decisions to parents. When more control is yielded to the consumers of education, those who presumably have the best knowledge of the educational needs and desires of the children are allowed to use that knowledge in selecting a school. Because most parents believe that they know what is best for their children, it is difficult, politically, to argue against this position.

Finally, and probably most importantly, public schools, especially urban schools, are commonly perceived to be in such a sorry state that many people are willing to try any program that might help improve them. It is widely reported that U.S. children consistently rank lower than those of many other industrialized countries on international tests in mathematics and science.[12] And, as these reports have proliferated, expenditures for education in the U.S. have increased greatly. Total K–12 expenditures per pupil, in real current dollars, increased 35 percent in the 1970s and 33 percent in the 1980s. Throwing money at the problem seems not to have led to any clear improvements. Quite simply, many people have become fed up with the current system.

A CASE AGAINST SCHOOL CHOICE

The major concern of those who oppose school choice is the potential for inequities in a voucher program. The danger of a voucher plan is that there could be a significant movement of students from public to private schools, resulting in a loss of tax support and lower per-pupil expenditures in public schools. Vouchers would probably cover only a portion of tuition at many private schools. For instance, the recent California amendment offered a voucher worth $2,600, a figure less than half the statewide average for private-school tuition. Thus, even under a voucher plan, the majority of private schools would continue to attract students from families with above average incomes and would remain out of reach for many lower-income families. If this were to happen, public schools could end up becoming "dumping grounds" for disadvantaged students.

Parents might also choose their children's schools for the wrong reasons. For school choice to lead to improvements, the competition between schools should be based on educational quality. However, past evidence provided by Charles Clotfelter and new evidence that will be cited later suggest that, rather than the quality of a school, its racial composition may be an important factor in parental decisions to send their children to private schools. Hence, choice could lead to greater segregation without improving overall educational outcomes. Vouchers may also open the door for discrimination because private schools are not required by law to accept all students who apply for admission. Finally, some people simply object to school choice because it is offered as a false panacea that will distract attention from the real problems of funding and equity that now exist in the public schools.

EMPIRICAL EVIDENCE

We can distinguish two types of empirical evidence that bear on the school-choice debate: indirect and direct evidence. The indirect evidence comes from research done in situations similar to school-choice experiments, but not on the actual school districts where school choice has taken place. Generally, this research measures the achievement levels of students in public versus private schools. The direct evidence comes from the relatively few school-choice experiments that have been implemented in the United States. How these data are interpreted or valued depends on one's theoretical perspective.

INDIRECT EMPIRICAL EVIDENCE

Studies of the achievement differences between students at public and private schools are numerous. These data would make a compelling argument to many in the market-economy school and to some in the liberal tradition, while critical pedagogues would not be impressed. Nonetheless, several studies find that private schools are more effective than public schools.[13] These studies are controversial and have generated questions regarding such problems as the focus on standardized-test scores as the performance measure, the sensitivity of results to the choice of independent variables, results that were statistically significant but perhaps not substantively significant, and, perhaps most important, the problem of selection bias.

Recent contributors to the study of public versus private-school performance are aware of these problems and have addressed some or all of them. Evans and Schwab examine the data presented in *High School and Beyond*, but focus on the probability of finishing high school and entering higher education, rather than on gains in test scores. With other factors being held constant, Catholic-school students have a 12 percent higher probability of finishing high school and a 14 percent higher probability of entering higher education than do public-school students.[14] Sander finds that Catholic grade schools produce higher vocabulary, mathematics, and reading scores, but the same science scores as public schools. Curiously, however, this positive impact of Catholic schools is driven by non-Catholic students in Catholic schools. Goldhaber finds that private schools do not use resources more efficiently to produce higher test scores than public schools. Rather, the difference in test scores in favor of private schools is due to characteristics of the students and the schools' resources.[15] Toma took advantage of the variety of financing and provision combinations observed internationally to examine their impact on a standardized mathematics examination. She found that in the United States, Belgium, and New Zealand, the private schools outperformed the public schools. No difference was found in Canada or France.[16] Dingdon examined data from India and reported that the privately funded schools outperformed both the publicly funded schools and the publicly funded and regulated, but nominally private, schools on reading and mathematics tests. Neal examined graduation rate, rates of advancement to postsecondary education, and wages, and found that the superior performance by Catholic schools is evident primarily for urban minority students. He attributed this difference to the low quality of the public alternative.[17] In summary, the weight of evidence in the newer set of studies suggest superior performance in private schools.

Private schools are usually shown to be less costly than public schools. For example, Lott reports that public-school teachers are paid 20 percent more than their private-school counterparts, and that the operating expenditures of public schools exceed those of private schools by 80 percent.[18]

Based on another source, public-school teachers are paid 50 percent more than private-school teachers. Tuition data provide a convenient estimate of the cost of operating a private school. Recent average tuition figures are as follows: $2,138 for elementary schools, $4,578 for secondary schools, $4,266 for combined schools, and an overall average of approximately $5,000 for districts with 20,000 or more students. Levin, however, is circumspect about private- and public-school cost comparisons. One reason for this is that differences in the service mix increase the relative cost of public schools. Tuition may not include costs that are included in public-school costs. These might include textbooks and supplies, transportation, and additional fees for specialized services. Also, tuition underestimates costs insofar as contributions and endowments are used to reduce tuition. Hoxby reports that 56 percent of Catholic elementary-school income and 19 percent of Catholic secondary-school income are from these sources.[19]

DIRECT EMPIRICAL EVIDENCE

The history of tentative, geographically limited steps towards school choice in the United States began in the 1970s with the Alum Rock, California, voucher demonstration. As noted earlier, this experiment operationalized Christopher Jencks' liberal-tradition voucher theory. Parents in voucher-school attendance areas were allowed to choose among several "minischools," alternative educational programs organized within schools, and during the five years of the experiment, the number of programs increased from 22 in 6 schools to 51 in 14 schools. These parents were allowed to choose among programs in any voucher school; parents and students in nonvoucher-school areas were treated as controls. For voucher participants, free transportation was provided to non-neighborhood schools, and transfers were permitted during the year. Students who attended in the past or who had siblings enrolled in a given school were granted preferential access. A lottery was used to assign admissions to oversubscribed programs.[20]

Given that it was an experiment, the Alum Rock voucher plan was studied using a systematic, across-time research strategy. Surveys administered during the demonstration showed that voucher parents were consistently more knowledgeable about program options, transportation, and transfer rights than those who did not participate. Parents with children in voucher schools were more satisfied with their schools than in the past. Parental appreciation may have followed from the substance of the new programs or simply from being offered a choice, but whatever the reason, the opportunity to choose seems to have been welcomed.

Although closely monitored, the results of the Alum Rock experiment were mixed in terms of student performance and provided no basis for supporting or criticizing voucher initiatives. Results from the California state testing program showed a decline in voucher-student reading scores compared with their own age-adjusted performance prior to the experiment. Scores also dropped in comparison to the scores of students in nonvoucher schools. However, results from the metropolitan achievement test (MAT) showed that voucher students' scores increased about as much as those of students in Alum Rock Title I schools (i.e., schools eligible for federal funding to help poor children) who received the same test. Other evidence regarding student behavior was more positive. Unexcused absence rates dropped slightly for voucher-school students during the demonstration, and student attitudes towards school also appeared to improve.

Following the Alum Rock trial, many other school districts experimented with school-choice schemes, frequently relying on a small number of alternative schools and magnet schools to break the usual procedures for matching students with schools. But it would be incorrect to conclude much from this research. Access to these specialty programs and magnet schools is often highly competitive and restrictive. An important exception, however, is District 4, located in the Harlem area of New York city.

Another voucher program in the liberal tradition, the factors shaping the District 4 of today can be traced back to the late 1960s. Then, the administration of New York City's public-school system was decentralized to allow for greater local control. In 1972, the district consisted of 22 schools. But during the late 1970s and 1980s, about 30 alternative schools were developed so that over 50 schools now exist. After 1982, all families of incoming seventh-graders had the opportunity to choose a school. There have been no systematic studies of the effects of school choice in District 4, although some analyses have been conducted and the results have been widely discussed. In the early 1970s, the district was ranked the lowest in the city for mathematics and reading scores. Although some controversy surrounds test-score measures, student performance in the district appears to have improved significantly over performance in the district before changes started being made in the mid-1970s. Schools in District 4 also seem to enjoy greater levels of parental involvement than schools in districts with less well-developed choice programs. Thus, District 4 has received much critical acclaim from outside observers. For instance, Chubb and Moe, both liberal theorists, have suggested, "If there is a single school district in the country that deserves to be held up as a model for all others, it is East Harlem."[21]

Since the late 1980s, there have been many proposals for greater use of publicly funded vouchers. All but two of these proposals had been defeated until school choice was approved in Milwaukee (1994) and Cleveland (1996). The Milwaukee parental-choice program probably comes closest to approximating the voucher model that Friedman had in mind, although it is not nearly as universal as he envisioned. Because these plans are aimed primarily at urban student populations, they would also possess many of the characteristics espoused by theorists in the liberal tradition and the critical pedagogues.

The program provides an opportunity for students meeting specific criteria to opt out of the Milwaukee public schools and attend private schools in the city. Recently, this opportunity has been extended to religiously affiliated nonpublic schools. Students must come from households with an income less than 1.75 times the poverty level. They may not have been in private schools or in a school district other than the Milwaukee school district in the previous year. In selecting students, the schools cannot discriminate on the basis of race, religion, gender, prior achievement, or prior behavioral records. If a school is oversubscribed, selection must be made randomly. Further, choice students can make up a maximum of 49 percent of the student body. No more than 1 percent of the total student population can enroll in a given year. The choice students receive the state's contribution to the cost per student to carry with them to the private school.

The Milwaukee parental-choice program has been evaluated by political scientist John Witte and his associates at the University of Wisconsin at Madison. Over the course of a five-year study, Witte has traced five outcome measures: (1) achievement-test results; (2) attendance data; (3) parental attitudes; (4) parental involvement; (5) attrition from the program.[22] To analyze achievement-test results, Witte matched students in the choice program with a random sample of students from low-income households enrolled in the Milwaukee public schools. He then performed cohort tests, as well as analyses of the variance scores of the test performance of individual students. As a preliminary point, Witte observed that the students coming into the choice program were clearly behind average Milwaukee public-school students and also behind a large random sample of low-income students. From the cohort tests, which do not report the same students from year to year, Witte concluded that, in reading and mathematics, there was no significant difference between choice students and public-school students.

However, in the areas of attendance, parental involvement, and parental attitudes, Witte found a significant difference in favor of the choice schools, which would appeal to the liberal-tradition and critical-pedagogy theorists. In summary, then, his study demonstrated that there was improvement at the choice schools in nonacademic areas, but not in the academic areas studied, which disappoints the liberal-tradition theorists. But, as market-economy theorists are quick to point out, even though both student samples achieved at the same rate, the choice group did so at a significantly lower cost to the taxpayer, i.e., even though vouchers were academically neutral, they cost less.

THE MINNESOTA CHOICE PLAN

In 1987, Minnesota introduced a statewide public-school-only choice plan, allowing students to attend any school district, subject to space limitations and adherence to desegregation plans. The Minnesota plan was developed in the liberal tradition, especially influenced by Mario Fantini's principles. Although some analysis has been undertaken, there has been no systematic effort to evaluate the Minnesota initiative by making comparisons across experimental and control groups of students and parents. Thus, no information is available on the changes in individual students' academic performance that might have occurred as a result of exercising school choice. During the 1989–90 school year, however, Tenbusch conducted a survey of parents who had exercised their choice option and those who had not. He found parents to be "active" enrollment decision makers, regardless of whether they chose their local schools or exercised their choice option.[23] He also found that parents who exercised the choice option tended to be more highly educated than those who did not, and that they tended to have more influence than others with school administrators. Delaney analyzed the reasons why parents of gifted and talented children exercised the choice option in Minnesota. He concluded that the option was used primarily because they anticipated that their children's needs would be better met and that their children would receive more personal attention in the choice schools.[24] Law reported similar results from a more limited study.[25] Ysseldyke found that parents of students with disabilities who exercised their choice option also did so because they anticipated that their children's needs would be better met and their children would receive more personal attention in the choice schools. Analyzing aggregate statistics, Colopy and Tarr concluded that use of the enrollment option has increased with time, and that minority students and families use school choice at the same rate as white students and families. The authors also found that use of open enrollment is more likely in smaller districts, suburban and rural districts, and higher-poverty districts.[26] These findings are particularly appealing to the liberal-tradition and critical-pedagogy theorists.

Tenbusch found in a survey of school principals that open enrollment has stimulated changes in curricula and support services in schools and promoted more parent and teacher involvement in school planning and decision making. It has also increased the ethnic and cultural diversity of schools.[27] Funkhouser and Colopy reported findings from interviews with school administrators in districts that had lost the most students through open enrollment and a set of comparison districts. They found that districts losing large numbers of students were more likely to take steps to attract students and to discourage others from leaving than districts that had few losses and few gains and those districts that had net gains in students.[28] Once again, these data dismiss some of the objections of opponents of school choice and bolster the case of the liberal theorists and critical pedagogues who advocate school choice.

The Minnesota open-enrollment plan has proven to be an influential policy innovation. Since 1987, over forty state legislatures have considered a similar form of school choice, and variations of the Minnesota approach have been adopted by at least eighteen other states. While it is true that the Minnesota approach seems a pale shadow of the plans proposed by Friedman and Chubb and Moe, it is important to recognize that, in combination, the various choice approaches now operating in the state are changing the way that public education is delivered. Further, these approaches raise important questions for parents, such as whether to exercise their choice options and what schools to consider if they are making a choice. Although Minnesota has had the longest statewide experience of school choice, and although it has been the focus of considerable research and media attention, many important questions about school choice remain to be addressed using evidence from this state. For example, longitudinal research designs could be used to explore the long-term behavior and attitudes of parents and students making use of the open-enrollment option, compared with those who do not. Similar designs could also be used to explore the short-term changes that schools make as a consequence of losing or attracting students and the longer-term sustainability of these changes. Studies could also explore whether open enrollment has led to a decline in the use of private school as a means of avoiding local public schools.

NEW INDIRECT EMPIRICAL EVIDENCE

There are a number of educational voucher programs now being implemented, including those in Cleveland, Ohio, Arizona, and, most recently, Florida. However, these plans are too recent for any direct empirical evidence worth noting to be cited.

Although it does not directly involve school-choice students, Dan Goldhaber, a research analyst with the CNA Corporation, has recently conducted a related study that may be helpful in assessing the viability of school-choice programs.[29] The underlying assumptions made by many of those who support school choice are (1) that nonpublic schools are more efficient than public schools, (2) that parents can distinguish between schools of differing quality, and (3) that parents will select schools that perform well. In 1997, Goldhaber completed a study of a nationwide sample of public- and private-high-school students, using data drawn from the National Educational Longitudinal Study (NELS) of 1988, which addresses these issues. He found the evidence mixed with regard to these hypotheses.

The NELS data set is based on a survey conducted by the National Center for Education Statistics (NCES). NCES sampled more than 20,000 eighth-graders nationwide, many of whom were surveyed again in the tenth and twelfth grades, NELS includes teacher, administrator, parent, and student responses on a variety of survey questions. At several points, NELS administered standardized tests in math, reading, history, and science. In addition, NELS is unique in that it allows students to be linked directly to their particular classes and teachers. For example, it is possible to determine the actual class size for a particular student, rather than just an aggregate measure, such as the average pupil-teacher ratio in the school, which is typically the case in other data sets.

In the sample for this study, Goldhaber drew school teacher and class information from NELS first follow-up survey (1990) and student and family-background variables from both the base year (1988) survey and the first follow-up. He focused on achievement in the tenth-grade reading and mathematics standardized tests. The main sample consisted of 3,347 tenth-graders, of whom 451 were in private schools. The reading/English sample consisted of 3,190 students, of whom 399 attended private schools. Students in private schools tended to come from families with better-educated parents who had substantially higher incomes than those in the public-school sample. In addition, the parents of private-school children had already demonstrated an interest in their children's education by choosing to pay for nonpublic schooling.

On average, the private-school students outscored their public-school counterparts by 7.5 points on the tenth-grade test in mathematics and by 3.8 points on the reading test. However, the fact that the parents had consciously chosen private schools brings up an important statistical problem in trying to determine how effective private schools are relative to public schools. Known as selection bias, this phenomenon may occur when there are important unobservable characteristics of students that influence achievement and are systematically related to the school sector in which the student is enrolled. These characteristics might include student motivation or the educational environment of the home. Selection bias can easily have come into play in this study, and may have accounted for many of the differences observed.

In Goldhaber's analysis, he estimated four models of educational achievement based on standardized math and reading tests in public and private schools. These achievement models employ an education production function methodology, in which achievement in the tenth grade is modeled as a function of eighth-grade achievement, student and family-background variables, schooling variables, and correction for selection bias.

The results of these achievement models were used to answer questions about the relative efficiency of public schools, as opposed to non-public schools. If the arguments for the greater efficiency of private schools are accurate, we should observe a higher return on schooling resources in the private sector than in the public sector. Put another way, we might find that a teacher teaching a given set of students in the private sector would be more effective than that same teacher teaching the same set of students in a public school with comparable resources. Statistical tests fail to confirm this hypothesis. In fact, corrected differentials, which show what a given student would have achieved in tenth grade had he or she been attending a school in the alternative sector and brought all schooling characteristics along, show that much of the raw mean difference between sectors disappears when a comparison is made between students of equal ability who have teachers and classmates with similar characteristics. Controlling for differences in individuals, families, and schooling resources, Goldhaber found no case in which there is a statistically significant effect of private schools on math and reading test scores.

Although private-school students have higher mean test scores than public-school students, the great majority of the mean differences between school sectors can be attributed to differences in the characteristics of students attending schools in those sectors rather than to differences in the effectiveness of these schools. Essentially, private schools attract students who are from better-educated, wealthier families and who enter school with above-average standardized test scores. These are students who would do well in both private and public schools.

These findings imply that with a given set of schooling resources, there is no reason to believe that an average private school would do a better job of educating a group of students than an average public school would do with that same group of students. However, it is important to note that parents making these choices very often encounter situations where there are marked differences in the resources available to each school.

To determine whether parents do, in fact, select schools based on educational quality, achievement differentials can be calculated that incorporate differences between the sectors in school resources, student bodies, and so on. These achievement differentials can be used to estimate a model of public- or private-school choice. The hypothesis is that parents are more likely to send their children to private school when estimated private-school achievement is greater than the public school's, and the probability grows as that gap increases. Conversely, they are more likely to send their children to public school when estimated public-school achievement exceeds estimated private-school achievement, and the probability grows as the gap increases. Also included in this model are controls for family background and for the racial and income composition of the schools in each sector—concerns of the liberal theorists and the critical pedagogues.

The results of the study show that parents, as expected, respond to these differences in estimated achievement. They are more likely to send their children to private schools as private-sector achievement rises relative to public-sector achievement. Thus, parents appear to be educated consumers in the sense that they select schools that benefit their children academically. This finding tends to support the proponents of school choice, like Friedman, Chubb and Moe, and Jencks, who argue that choice would create competition between schools based on school quality.[30]

CONSTITUTIONAL ISSUES

Another issue that is often brought forward by opponents of tuition vouchers is their alleged unconstitutionality. However, the most current court decisions seem to indicate that vouchers may well be found constitutional. The case that bears most relevance to the debate over vouchers is *Lemon v. Kurtzman*. In this case the Supreme Court set forth a test by which future cases regarding government aid to nonpublic schools would be judged in light of their compliance with the provisions of the Establishment Clause of the First Amendment to the U.S. Constitution. The Establishment Clause precludes the establishment of a religion by the state. The Lemon test is three pronged, but a law need violate only one of the three to be found in violation of the Establishment Clause. The first step in the test asks whether the law has a secular purpose; the second asks if the laws' primary effect is to advance or inhibit religion, and the third step asks if there is excessive entanglement between the church and the state.

Milwaukee's school voucher program has been operating for nearly a decade. Initially, the city only allowed vouchers to be used to send students to nonreligious private schools. In 1995, however, the Wisconsin legislature voted to include religious schools in the program. But the expansion was put on hold after it was challenged in court.

On June 10, 1998, the Wisconsin supreme court ruled that incorporating religious schools into the program did not violate either the state constitution or the U.S. Constitution. Using the Lemon test, the court said the program's origin was driven largely by a secular purpose—to expand educational opportunities for poor children. Additionally, the court noted, any child attending a parochial school under the program could be excused from religious instruction if his or her parents requested such an exemption.[31]

The American Civil Liberties Union, People for the American Way, and affiliates of the state's largest teachers' unions appealed the decision to the U.S. Supreme Court. Both supporters and opponents hoped a Supreme Court ruling would clarify what many view as a host of confusing and contradictory decisions on state support of religious schools. The Supreme Court did so on June 27, 2002, when it ruled that tuition vouchers are constitutional.

POLICY IMPLICATIONS AND CONCLUSIONS

What do all of these findings tell us? Both the direct and indirect evidence yields mixed results. There is no compelling empirical evidence that leads us to believe that school choice in any form will be a panacea for addressing the problems in our schools. On the other hand, to expect empirical evidence from such short-lived programs to be compelling is unreasonable. What we can reasonably conclude, however, is that school choice, where it has been implemented, has not had the catastrophic results that some opponents have predicted. In fact, there have been some very encouraging signs that both public and nonpublic schools alike have been improved by the process. I know first hand that needed change takes place much more readily when the Sword of Damocles is hanging overhead. I can remember instances where teachers could not possibly find the time to give students more individual attention, or when suggested changes in teaching methodologies were mightily resisted. But when the same school was in danger of closing, suddenly the same teachers found more time to devote to their at-risk students, and suddenly they began to adapt their teaching styles to the learning styles of their students.

In the September 15, 1999, issue of *Education Week*, a front page headline read, "Schools Hit by Vouchers Fight Back." The article speaks of changes that have occurred at the Spencer Bibbs Advanced Learning Academy in Florida as a result of competition from voucher schools. Spencer Bibbs has incorporated a new dress code, as well as other more curricular and instructional changes. "The new dress code is a visible reminder of the less tangible changes staff members at Spencer Bibbs have made following their recent branding by the state as a failing school."[32] But Bibbs also became one of only two Florida schools where students were offered vouchers to attend another public or private school of their choice. So, as much as they loathe the new state policy, staff members say that they are determined to overcome the stigma and improve in the future. Interesting, isn't it, what creating a little sense of urgency in an institution can do. This incident at Spencer Bibbs Advanced Learning Academy leads me to believe that a carefully crafted school-choice program could be an important component, albeit only one of several, in a much-needed and multifaceted plan for education reform that would benefit public and nonpublic schools alike.

What I have chosen to suggest is an approach that grows out of both the liberal (Ignatian vision) and critical-pedagogy traditions. The tension for me is that as an administrator, a market-driven approach is attractive, but as an educator, the liberal-tradition and critical-pedagogy models are preferable. As an administrator, I would like to see the broadest possible population benefit from a reform like school choice.

In this role I would call for an all-inclusive school-choice plan driven by market forces, which would make vouchers available to all students. However, as an educator, I am concerned about pedagogy, equity, fairness, ethics, democracy, and serving the underserved. For these reasons, I much prefer to concentrate our limited resources where they can do the most good. Therefore, I am suggesting a modified or limited plan in which only the most needy would benefit.

I would suggest, then, that a school-choice plan be structured according to the liberal and critical-pedagogy traditions mentioned earlier. It should concern itself with cultural, societal, and racial matters and be as inclusive as possible. It should also concern itself with economic stratification, the distribution of power, and the implied moral imperatives. Therefore, any proposed school-choice plan should sound a caution regarding the equity consequences of choice. We cannot allow school-choice plans to resegregate our schools, although we are currently far from truly integrating them.

Many educational researchers and practitioners suggest that our public schools are underfunded, and that if adequate funding were provided, many of the schools' alleged shortcomings would be eliminated. For example, if funds were available to support a class size limit of ten students, the at-risk and special learners could be given the attention that they need and achievement scores might significantly increase. I do not doubt the wisdom of this view. However, the chances of the American public making available the considerable amount of incremental revenue needed to accomplish the above are slim at best. Increased funding of public education does not seem to be something that will happen anytime soon. In the absence of any significant increase in funding for public schools, the school-choice plan suggested here may be one of the few alternatives acceptable to most taxpayers to improve our schools. If it does not work, the argument for increased funding of public schools might become more palatable to the American taxpayer.

Studies also show that upper-income families are clearly more likely to send their children to private schools.[33] Thus, these families would be likely beneficiaries of any voucher plan like the one proposed in California. The $2,600 California voucher would probably have been too small to enable low-income families to afford high-quality private schools, but it would clearly have benefited those families whose children are already enrolled in the private sector or those upper-income families for whom $2,600 would be enough incentive to tip the scale in favor of private schooling. In my view, this type of voucher plan would not meet the standards of the critical theorists. One way to counter the potential for greater economic stratification in a voucher plan would be to create a progressive voucher program. Progressiveness could be achieved by simply targeting the voucher to low-income families (as is the case in the Milwaukee plan) or by creating a sliding scale so that the size of the voucher would vary with income or with the amount of private-school tuition.

Finally, let us discuss the implications that vouchers would have on the distribution of power in American education. Critical theorists concern themselves with the contradictions that occur in education. For example, the American belief in equality is in contradiction with the simultaneous promotion of practices that create inequality among various groups. Although its goal is equality, I concur with the critical theorists in believing that the current distribution of power in American education has led to an inequality whereby our most needy students are being marginalized and underserved.

Currently, the power in American education is concentrated in the hands of politicians, boards of education, educational administrators, and unions. Although well meaning, some of these decision makers have virtually excluded the parents and their children from any meaningful input into their process and, as a result, have marginalized an entire stratum of people. Among the most underrepresented groups in the education decision-making process are the parents of at-risk, minority, and low-income children. In my view, a finely crafted school-choice program, limited to low-income families, would redistribute power by placing it in the hands of parents, giving them a chance to determine which educational setting best meets their children's needs.

Many of the current educational reform movements call for more parental involvement in school. No politically correct member of the public-school establishment would speak against such a proposition. But the irony is that the very same advocates of parental involvement would likely be opponents of school choice. In my view, school choice is the epitome of parental involvement.

This book speaks to the need to examine American education through the dual lenses of critical theory and the Ignatian tradition.

These ideals imply that the individual, no matter what his or her racial background, gender, or socioeconomic status, should be integrally involved in the shaping of public education. Applying these ideals to education requires students and their parents to have a determining voice in where and how they are educated. For all of its significant contributions to American democracy, our current monolithic public-school educational process has not attained the democratic ideal. The modified or mitigated school-choice initiative in the critical-pedagogy and liberal traditions that we are considering here would get us closer to the democratic ideal of affording more parents and their children the opportunity and ability to decide which type of school, public or nonpublic, best meets their educational needs. The economically advantaged already have that opportunity. The proposed school-choice program would extend that opportunity to the poor and move us ever closer to full inclusiveness and the democratic ideal.

In conclusion, it is my hope that the contents of this chapter will demonstrate how educational-policy decisions can be developed and placed into effective practice by utilizing the theoretical underpinnings of critical theory and the Ignatian vision. It is also my hope that this chapter will stimulate and enlighten the continuing discourse on the important issue of school choice. Perhaps, school choice will make no substantial difference in how our young people progress academically. But, at least the decision will be in the hands of those who have most at stake. As it is now, we are not very successful in educating our low-income, at-risk students, but it is people other than their parents who are making the decisions that affect their lives. Our limited experience with school choice indicates that it can make a difference in the schooling of our most needy young people. So, why not give it the serious consideration it deserves?

NOTES

1. A. Molnar et al., "Research, Politics, and the School-Choice Agenda," *Phi Delta Kappan* 78(3) 1996: 240–243.

2. T. Parry, "Theory Meets Reality in the Education Voucher Debate: Some Evidence from Chile," *Education Economics* 5(3) 1997: 307–331.

3. Milton Friedman, "The Role of Government in Education," *Economics and the Public Interest* (December 1955): 127–134.

4. Milton Friedman, "The Role of Government in Education," *Economics and the Public Interest* (December 1955): 127–134.

5. John Coons and Stephen Sugarman, *Education by Choice: The Case for Family Control* (Berkeley: University of California Press, 1978).

6. Mario Fantini, *Public Schools of Choice* (New York: Simon and Schuster, 1973).

7. Robert H. Palestini, "Educational Choice and the Politics of Inclusion," *Catholic Education: A Journal of Inquiry and Practice* 5(1) September 2001: 6–27.

8. John Chubb and Terry Moe, *Politics, Markets, and America's Schools* (Washington, DC: The Brookings Institute, 1990).

9. Herbert Gintis, *Unconventional Wisdom: Essay in Honor of John Kenneth Galbraith* (New York: Houghton Mifflin, 1989).

10. Herbert Gintis, "The Political Economy of Choice," *Teachers College Record* 96(3) 1995: 492–511.

11. A. Downs, *An Economic Theory of Democracy* (New York: Harper Brothers, 1951).

12. E. Hanuschek, "The Economics of Schooling: Production and Efficiency in Public Schools," *Journal of Economic Literature* 24 (January 1996): 1141–1178.

13. James Coleman and Thomas Hoffer, *Public and Private Schools: The Impact on Communities* (New York: Basic Books, 1987).

14. W. N. Evans and R. M. Schwab, "Finishing High School and Starting College: Do Catholic Schools Make a Difference?" *The Quarterly Journal of Economics* 110 (75) 1996: 941–975.

15. D. Goldhaber, "Public and Private High Schools: Is School Choice an Answer to the Productivity Problem?" *Economics of Education Review* 15(12) 1996: 93–109.

16. E. F. Toma, "Public Funding and Private Schooling Across Countries," *Journal of Law and Economics* 34(96) 1996: 121–148.

17. D. Neal, "The Effects of Catholic Secondary Education on Educational Achievement," *Journal of Labor Economics* 15(1) 1997: 98–123.

18. R. J. Lott, Jr., "An Explanation for Public Provision of Schooling: The Importance of Indoctrination," *Journal of Law and Economics* 33 (1990): 199–231.

19. C. M. Hoxby, "Are Efficiency and Equity in School Finance Substitutes or Complements?" *Journal of Economic Perspectives* 10(4) 1996: 51–52.

20. D. Lamdin and J. Mintrom, "School Choice in Theory and Practice: Taking Stock and Looking Ahead," *Education Economics* 5(3) 1997: 211–344.

21. John Chubb and Terry Moe, "America's Public Schools: Choice or Panacea," *The Brookings Review* 91(97) 1991: 4–13.

22. J. F. Witte, "Private school versus public school: Are there findings that should affect the educational choice debate," *Economics of Education Review* 11(92) 1992: 371–394.

23. J. P. Tenbusch, Parent Choice Behavior Under Minnesota's Open Enrollment Program. Paper presented at the annual meeting of the American Education Research Association, Atlanta, GA, April 1993.

24. Thomas Delaney, "Participation of Rural Students with Disabilities and Rural Gifted Students in Open Enrollment," *Rural Special Education Quarterly* 14(3) 1995: 31–35.

25. M. Y. Law, "The Participation of Students Who Are Enrolled As Gifted and Talented in Minnesota's Open Enrollment Option," *Journal for the Education of the Gifted* 17(94) 1994: 276–298.

26. K. W. Colopy and H. C. Tarr, *Minnesota's Public School Choice Options* (Washington, DC: U.S. Department of Education/Policy Studies Associates, 1994).

27. J. P. Tenbusch, Parent Choice Behavior Under Minnesota's Open Enrollment Program. Paper presented at an annual meeting of the American Education Research Association, Atlanta, GA, April 1993.

28. J. E. Funkhouser and K. W. Colopy, *Minnesota's Open Enrollment Option: Impacts on School Districts* (Washington, DC: U.S. Department of Education/Policy Studies Associates, 1994).

29. Dan Goldhaber, "Public and Private High Schools: Is School Choice an Answer to the Productivity Problem," *Economics of Education Review* 15(12) 1996: 93–109.

30. E. Hanuschek, "The Economics of Schooling: Production and Efficiency in Public Schools," *Journal of Economic Literature* 24 (January 1996): 1141–1178.

31. Robert H. Palestini and Karen Palestini, *Law and American Education* (Lanham, MD: The Scarecrow Press, 2001).

32. J. L. Sandham, "Schools Hit by Vouchers Fight Back," *Education Week* (September 15, 1999): 20–21.

33. W. D. Hawley, "The Predictable Consequences of School Choice," *Education Week* 56 (April 10, 1996): 47.

Index

accommodation, 78
Adorno, Theodor, 25
Alderfer, E., 60
Alum Rock, 143, 152
Arrupe, Pedro, 44
avoidance, 78

Benjamin, Walter, 25
Bolman, L. and T. Deal, 7–9
bounded rationality, 31
brainstorming, 85
Brookings Institute, 144
Bruner, Jerome, 58

Carlson, Richard, 105
change, 93, 95–136
choice, 138–65
Chubb, John, 144
classical theory, 51
Cleveland Plan, 139
Clotfelter, Charles, 150
Coleman, John, 144
collaboration, 78
communication, 65–75
compromise, 78
conflict management, 76–80
contingency theory, 7, 127

Coons, John, 142
covenant, 117
critical theory, 2–4, 23–33, 37
culture, 53–56
cura personalis, 40, 43, 48

decision making, 80–86
Delphi technique, 86, 112
Deming, Edwards, 96
De Pree, Max, 35
Dewey, John, 17, 30
discernment, 40, 48
Dreeden, K., 15
Durkheim, R., 15

Eisenhower, Dwight, 92
empowerment, 89, 120
equity theory, 61
Erickson, 37
expectancy theory, 62–64

Fantini, Mario, 142
feedback, 65–67
force field analysis, 104, 106
forcing, 78
Foucault, Michel, 27
Frankford School, 25

Freire, Paulo, 27
Friedman, Milton, 140
Fromm, Erich, 25
functionalism, 5, 12–21, 39

Gintis, Herbert, 146
Giroux, Henry, 28
Glasser, William, 58
Goldhaber, Dan, 157
Gramsci, Antonio, 26
Greenleaf, Robert, 32, 100
Griffiths, D., 20, 37

Habermas, Jurgen, 27
Hanson, Mark, 98
Hawthorne Effect, 1
heroes, 135
Herzberg's theory, 60
Horkheimer, Max, 25
human capital theorists, 19
human resource frame, 7

Ignatian vision, 2–6, 40–49, 57

Jefferson, Thomas, 17
Jencks, Christopher, 142, 152
Jesuit, 40, 43, 44
Johari Window, 68

Kolvenbach, Peter-Hans, 44

Lam, Diana, 9
leadership, 4–11, 56–57
Lemon v. Kurtzman, 160

magis, 40, 42
Mann, Horace, 17
Marcuse, Herbert, 25
market economy, 140
Maslow, Abraham, 58, 59

matrix design, 72
McClelland's Trichotomy, 60
Merton, T., 15
Milwaukee Plan, 139
Minnesota Plan, 155
mission statement, 92
Moe, Terry, 144
Moore, John, 120
motivation, 58

negotiations, 90
nominal group technique, 112

open systems theory, 52, 126
Organizational Fairness
    Questionnaire, 62
ownership, 116

Peters and Waterman, 8
political frame, 8
Pope John Paul II, 44
positivist theory, 2–5, 12–21
post-positivist, 37
power, 87

Ross, Edward, 20

satisficing, 110
Senge, Peter, 54, 135
Sergiovanni, Thomas, 120
service, 40, 43–45
Simon, Herbert, 110
situational leadership, 7
Skinner, Albert, 58
social justice, 40, 46–47
social systems, 51, 125
staff development, 121
strategic planning, 91
structural frame, 8
structure, 51

Sugarman, Stephen 142

Taylor, Frederick, 1, 20
transformational leader, 10, 57
tuition vouchers 138–65

vouchers, 138–65
Vroom and Yetton, 80

Watson, Goodwin, 106
Witte, John, 154

About the Author

Robert Palestini is dean of Graduate and Continuing Studies at Saint Joseph's University in Philadelphia. He has spent almost forty years in basic and higher education. He has been a high-school biology and general-science teacher, a principal, assistant superintendent, and superintendent of schools. He is the author of four books on various topics in educational administration. In addition to being dean, Dr. Palestini teaches two education-leadership courses in the Ed.D. program in education at Saint Joseph's (rpalesti@sju.edu).